I Love Life

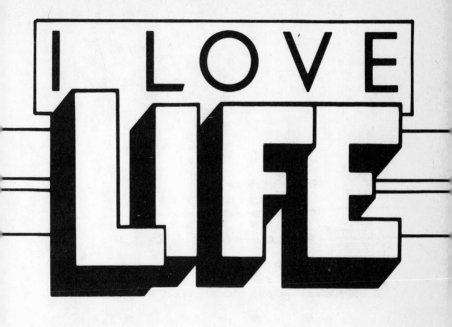

I LOVE LIFE

JERRY DAHMEN

BROADMAN PRESS
Nashville, Tennessee

© Copyright 1989 • Broadman Press
all rights reserved
4250-77

ISBN: 0-8054-5077-7
Dewey Decimal Classification: 920
Subject Heading: BIOGRAPHY - COLLECTED WORKS
Library of Congress Catalog Number: 88-30431

Printed in the United States of America

Library of Congress Cataloging-in-Publication Data

Dahmen, Jerry, 1949-
  I love life.

  1. Conduct of life.   2. Success.   I. Title.
  BJ1581.2.D27   1989   248.8′6   88-30431
  ISBN 0-8054-5077-7

Dedication

I Love Life is dedicated to a beautiful woman who touched thousands of lives. Mary Catherine Strobel was easily recognized in soup kitchens as she poured a cup of coffee for a stranger (who, within minutes, was her friend). When she wasn't helping out in a shelter for the poor, Mary Catherine was taking clothes to a needy family, placing flowers in sterile hospital rooms, even attending a funeral or two. Everybody, she told her children, was "my good friend."

Mary Catherine possessed charm, grace, beauty, and inner strength. The silver-haired activist for the homeless was a "giver." While so many of us search with great effort for happiness, love, and success in life, Mary Catherine had an abundance of each of them.

Service to mankind was her life-style. She willingly gave her time, her love, and her good humor. Mary Catherine also shared her faith. After each meal, her typical expression was "God bless everybody."

She would have liked the people in this book. But, just reading about them would not have been enough for her. She probably would have wanted to know everything about them and how she could help them in their lives. That's not surprising for a woman who truly loved life.

I Love Life would have been more than a title of a book for Mary Catherine. It was much more than that. Those three powerful words were a way of life for a wonderful and compassionate human being.

Acknowledgments

My thanks to these folks who have supported the "I Love Life" concept . . . Keith Bilbrey, Moon Mullins, Dan Haskell, Brent Stoker, Ted Cramer, Buddy Sadler, Bill Hance, Judy Mizell, Jim Farley, Frank Raphael, and Jerry Thompson. My gratitude to Patsy Donahoe and Tom Bryant for their assistance.

Thanks to Willard Scott, *Tennessean* Publisher John Seigenthaler and Executive Editor Sandra Roberts, Walter Anderson, Bob Dotson, Irving Dickman, and Earl Nightingale for their input.

Thanks to Opryland USA's E. W. Wendell and Tom Griscom and WSM's General Manager Bob Meyer for their support of "I Love Life."

And loving thanks to my wife Linda who has shared my dream for over a decade. She's a friend I am blessed to have.

Contents

Foreword

The news business is tricky. It serves an undeniable need, but it often tells us things we don't want to know . . . or at least things we just don't want to hear. In the process, the messenger often receives some of the ill will that actually belongs to the message itself.

Of course, not all news is bad, and those working in the news media don't really have to look very hard to find good news. More and more they seem to write about it and broadcast it. The good is just as much a reflection of society as is the bad.

Jerry Dahmen knows that. His credentials as a reporter of all kinds of news are excellent. He has won awards wherever he has worked—for topics his audiences wanted him to explore and also for topics his audiences would just as soon have ignored.

He has made a specialty of reporting about people who can be inspirations to all of us. By lifting them up in the media, they will lift up the rest of us. That is the basis of *I Love Life,* a book that indeed will help you to do exactly that.

Even though some well-known celebrities are here, the majority of the people in this book are not public figures. They are people who have happily found their place of service in life and in so doing have helped hold society together. They are the people who needed help and were fortunate enough to find it. In turn, they have become helpers, enriching the lives of those around them. Without exception, every person in this book has overcome adversity. And they are people who give more than they take.

There are life-changing lessons throughout *I Love Life.* I am proud that the radio version of *I Love Life* is on WSM, one of the nation's top stations and part of the company where Jerry Dahmen and I work.

I Love Life is encouraging, inspiring, and motivational. If you already love life, it can aid you to love it even more. If you don't love life, then this book may help you do that. And then you'll find out that life is genuinely worth living.

—E. W. Wendell
President and Chief
Executive Officer
Opryland USA Inc.

Introduction

Parkersburg, West Virginia—Authorities believe the decapitation murder of a thirty-four-year-old construction worker may have been a "drug-related" killing. The bound body of Charles Marsh of Columbia, South Carolina, was found on a bed in a rural house near Parkersburg. The victim's head was on a dresser . . .

Miami, Florida—A ten-year-old boy is charged with the fatal stabbing of an eight-year-old playmate who called him a sissy for refusing to play touch football . . .

Nashville, Tennessee—Eighteen-year-old Robert Howell has been indicted on four assault counts by the grand jury. Howell is accused of biting his infant son and breaking his ribs . . .

After being bombarded with those kinds of stories for years, a housewife from the Midwest, Mrs. Ann Peterson, couldn't take it anymore. She was angry and was not going to hide her feelings. She wrote me a letter that confirmed what I already realized. The letter was short, but direct:

Far too much radio and TV coverage is devoted to negative events, leaving positive happenings untouched. I'm not telling you to forget about violence, but could you please give me something positive? I know there are a lot of things you could cover. All I ask is a favor as a listener. Give the other side of the news a chance to be heard. I'm fed up with hearing about mass murders in Texas or the prediction of a recession or depression by some big-name economist. I doubt if this letter will make a difference, but at least I feel better by letting you know how I feel.

Good news, a label which encompasses stories of hope, inspiration, and courage, has been characterized by some media people as "fluff" and an escape from reality. That's a bad mistake. My longtime friend and ABC radio broadcaster Jim Farley believes networks understand the need for good news and are not shy about airing such stories. "It is a turn off to report story after story of murders and rapes," Jim told me. "When you get into a pattern of negative news, it's just too much, and people tune out. What we have to remember is what news is—the day-by-day adventures of the human race."

But what about the anchors, directors, and producers of the news media in New York and Washington? Do they agree with Jim? He answered, "News people are becoming more sensitive to what their audiences want and need. That includes a heavy dose of nice things, good things. That's why many television stations and even some networks do 'good-news' shows. It is also an attempt to answer those critics who say the news media focuses only on the bad. So we go out of our way to find the good-news stories. There's nothing wrong in a newscast being heartwarming. That's not a description that bothers me. I think it's absolutely appropriate.

"If you want to get a reaction from someone in the field," Jim suggested at the end of our conversation, "call Bill Wheatley of NBC-TV. He's an acquaintance of mine who happens to be the executive producer of 'NBC Nightly News.'" With help from Jim, I soon had Bill on the phone.

Interestingly enough, the day before Bill and I talked, the "Nightly News" featured a segment on Down's Syndrome children who were being adopted by "normal parents." It was not buried as a "kicker" story but was aired midway in the half-hour news show. As Bill and I talked I mentioned the piece, and Bill was excited about those kinds of positive human-interest stories.

"People overcoming adversity has always been a good news story and continues to be. In fact, here at 'NBC Nightly News' we are always looking for stories about people who make a difference . . . One of our reporters has developed that into a specialty.

During the course of a year, we do dozens of stories about the 'little' person in society who is perhaps overcoming a handicap or helping the handicapped. And that's all part of the news."

I felt even more motivated about the concept of "I Love Life" as we discussed good vs. bad news. I was still smarting from a conversation I had with a network news anchor several years earlier at a broadcasters convention in Dallas. "I love *what?*" he almost shouted at me as I tried to describe my upbeat show.

As I was sampling reactions about good news from radio and television specialists, I received a review copy of a book by Walter Anderson, the editor of *Parade* magazine. Entitled *Courage Is a Three-letter Word,* it told wonderful stories about many of America's most distinguished men and women who have overcome fears to achieve success.

Maybe if I contacted Mr. Anderson for an interview about his book, he wouldn't mind talking about the "good news" concept for my book. He should certainly know what the public wants. After all, the magazine he edits has the largest circulation ever with sixty-five million readers (more than any television network has viewers).

The following week I was on the phone to Walter Anderson. I explained my interest in his book about good news. "Human-interest stories have always worked," he emphasized from his New York office. "Horatio Alger lived a long time ago, and yet we refer to his stories today. Look at 'Roots,' the most-watched program in television history. A human-interest story. What about the Olympics? Human interest. Of course, it's that idea of challenge. We live this every day.

"I've been editor of *Parade* for eight years, and during that time, we've done thousands of human-interest stories. . . . They help us discover what we're interested in—each other and in ourselves. We know ourselves through others."

"So," I asked, "how do you decide what stories to present, considering the tremendous resources available to you, Mr. Anderson?"

"Every human being struggles from the first slap on the backside until the last heartbeat," he pointed out enthusiastically. "We all survive and endure until that last heartbeat. But a precious few do more than survive or endure. They prevail, and from their lives, we can find inspiration and live better ourselves."

I could not have agreed more! Body and soul, I am a newsperson.

In my early broadcast years, I was worn down covering rapes, murders, and political candidates who delight in attacking one another. Yet, I have been fortunate. "I Love Life" has given me a daily refresher course in basic human values—love, compassion, faith. These words are still powerful, even in our computerized and technological world. This is the practicality of *I Love Life*. This is not merely a "good news" book or a "how to" success manual. Many of those are already in the marketplace, offering instant "me" success. *I Love Life* is unique because it presents stories of men and women who possess qualities the "me" generation has yet to discover and put to use.

"I Love Life" has gone beyond a radio show or a book. It has grabbed hold of me and will not let me go. It started as a dream in broadcasting to make a concept work. It has become my mission! I believe in its power, authenticity, and sincerity. The supreme compliment I receive from people at my speaking engagements is: "I can feel the honesty and sincerity in the program." Also, "It's not hype." God gave me an idea and an ability to communicate, and I want to utilize both of them to the fullest. "I Love Life" doesn't analyze facts or graphs to put its message across. Its origin is in the heart.

Part I:
Children of Adversity

1
Encouragement:
My Story

"I was the kid who must have had a sign around his neck that read, 'I'm a victim!' That was the image I projected—and actually believed."

If I had listened to those who put me down when I was a child, I wouldn't be in broadcasting and making speeches. Neither would I be winning national media awards nor writing a book.

"Jerry," one of my elementary teachers scolded me, "you'll never be an achiever. You can't sound your vowels properly, you can't raise your hand when I ask a question, and you can't even write correctly" (I am left-handed, and she was convinced that was unacceptable in her class). The "I-can't" syndrome was pounded into my head, not only by some of my teachers, but my classmates as well. I was the kid who must have had a sign around his neck that read, "I'm a victim!" That was the image I projected —and actually believed.

As a youngster, I had this mental picture that a kid should be big and muscular, not skinny and awkward. I wasn't athletic in appearance and therefore wasn't interested in sports. Being the last kid picked on teams in gym class triggered a fear of rejection in me. "Hey," I was chided by the strong, muscular kids, "we don't want you with us."

Having no encouragement to participate in sports, I made every excuse I could think of to avoid them. When the classes would kick off, my blood pressure would skyrocket. I would always wind up with nosebleeds and wait out the class in the rest room where I would cough up blood. ("You're anemic," the school nurse reminded me. "Stay off the gym floor, and you'll be safe.)

I didn't mind the warning. After all, being alone, I surmised back then, was so much better than messing up in class! *Why try?*

I was convinced, *I'd never win at anything.* I knew I couldn't run as fast or perform as many pushups as the other kids. There I was—skin and bones, shorts always two sizes larger than I was. *Maybe I'll try a Charles Atlas Course,* I told myself. The picture in the Atlas advertisement (the big brute kicking sand into the puny little guy's face) warranted a last-ditch effort. But, by the time I received a reply from the Atlas people, my family doctor put a stop to gym class. "You're susceptible to nosebleeds, and participating in the classes will bring them on," he advised. "Go to study period instead."

Without any encouragement in pursuing sports, I was giving up on myself. I reasoned, *I'm not good at anything.* I felt inferior and inadequate. How badly I wanted to excel! That was a joke. I couldn't even be average, I reminded myself. I didn't like myself, and the image I put forth reflected what I believed. If I was called dumb by another kid, I never doubted his evaluation. *I must be dumb if someone tells me I am.* Unfortunately, the more I accepted the teasing, the more frequent and intense my antagonists became.

I dwelled on my imperfections. I wouldn't smile because I was so embarrassed that the gaps in my teeth would prompt ridicule. *If anyone sees them, I just know they'll make fun of me.* I even covered my nose with my hands when anyone stared at me. I was convinced it was the size of Jimmy Durante's snozz.

I had zero confidence in myself and didn't know how to break away from the fears that had immobilized me. While the other kids played together during recess, I was wandering in the school yard by myself. During class, I refused to raise my hand. That would be horrifying. *What if I don't have the right answer?* I reasoned. I was so scared I wouldn't even ask permission to go to the bathroom during class. *Everyone will stare at me. I'll just wait until the class ends.*

What could I do? I was scared to tell anyone what I was feeling. *Maybe I'm crazy and will be put away in a mental hospital, or maybe I'm to be the one who always is bullied and put down.* No one had even hinted that little Jerry could be an achiever and

believer. So, why should I have thought I could be? Without
self-esteem, saddled with speech difficulties and a small stature, I
hated myself. My thinking was narrow-minded and self-defeating.
*Everyone else has it better than me. Poor little me. I'm a loser and
always will be!*

My personality wasn't a hit with the teachers. They would
constantly remind me, "You need so much work with your conso-
nants and vowels," especially after I had attempted to read a prose
or poetry selection in class. "Perhaps your speech therapy classes
aren't working," one of them announced before the entire class.
"You had better get in gear and start trying, or you'll never make
it."

But I was trying! At least I felt I was. How much more could
I do? I would attend the special speech lessons until the seventh
grade. But I wasn't making much progress. What I was missing
could be summed up in one word: *encouragement!*

"Now, Jerry," one of the speech teachers would instruct me,
"stand upright and sound like a rooster."

You've got to be kidding, I chuckled to myself.

"Crow as loudly as you can," she commanded in a loud voice.
"Don't be shy. Just do it!"

I tried and tried. "Err-err-err-er-er," I sputtered out loud.

"Keep doing it," she ordered.

*Oh, no, what if someone hears me? Then I'm really gonna be
hassled!*

The door to the room was wide open, and I noticed the tiny
eyeballs peering at me from the hallway. Between breaths I could
hear the giggling. *I'm really in trouble now. I'm gonna get picked
on.*

After half an hour of rooster crowing (the purpose of which I
still do not understand), I slowly inched my way back to the
fourth-grade class. The teacher was handing out papers. I tried to
be "The Invisible Man" as I slid into my chair. *Boy, I made it!
What a scare!*

As I glanced at my homework, Ben, the big shot in the class,
was leering at me. In a slow, but persistent, tone, he started

crowing like a rooster: "Err-er-er-er-er," the muscular bully was repeating. I could have melted right there. *Why me? Why can't you leave me alone? I've got to get out of here!*

I grabbed my books and papers and ran as fast as I could out of the classroom and straight home. *I'm sick and tired of being picked on. Can't I do anything right?* I kept asking myself.

I Had a Dream

I wouldn't dare tell anyone my long-range plans. They would've laughed. Even a compassionate person may have commented, "You're only daydreaming, kid." But the dream would not die, and it became stronger as I advanced in school. *Someday,* I vowed, *I'll be a public speaker and radio announcer!* The goal was planted in my subconscious, and no one could steal it away from me. But how would I transform that dream into reality? I was a victim of my own shyness and timidity. How can a kid who has been afraid to ask permission to go to the bathroom, for fear of being noticed, ever be a speaker and media man? *If only I could tell someone,* I told myself. What a mistake!

I was in junior high and had the strictest English teacher known to mankind. Mr. Armstrong (not his real name) could easily have been in the military. He went by the book and oftentimes dealt out corporal (no pun intended) punishment. But the robust, bespectacled instructor had a powerful, resonant voice. His diction was perfect. *If only I could have what he has someday. Maybe he'll work with me after school if I ask him.*

I soon found out that encouragement, tenderness, and kindness were not his strong suits. After class, I shuffled up to his desk and timidly approached him. "Mr. Armstrong, I really want to be a good speaker and be on the radio when I'm older. I know I don't talk very well, but maybe you can help me."

"I appreciate what you're trying to do," he answered, "but I don't have the time outside of class. You'll be treated like every other student." End of discussion! His sterile response set me back. I tried to seek support and was cut off. *Where do I go from here?* I asked myself.

The following day, Mr. Armstrong marched to the front of the room and announced, "Class, we are studying *Hamlet* this week, and I want each of you to study these verses and recite them. The dates of your reading are included in the papers I'm handing out."

"Oh, no," I panicked, "I'll fail at that. I can't do that in front of the class. Everybody will laugh. Maybe Mr. Armstrong will give me a break."

When the bell rang, I waited for Mr. Armstrong as he was clearing off his desk. "Sir," I confided, "I'm really scared about the reading. May I have more time before you ask me to recite?"

"That's out of the question," he coldly reacted. "You're no different from anyone else."

"But," I pleaded, "I'm so scared of messing up. My head's pounding, and my stomach hurts. I just need more time!"

"Jerry," he rather curtly concluded, "you will recite two days from now. Don't be sick."

Fear seized control of me. My head throbbed like a turbojet, my throat was as dry as Death Valley, and sweat poured out on my face and hands. There was no way I could con myself out of the reading or, in retrospect, my "moment of truth," my "D-Day."

At home I pwacticed (that's how I pronounced *practiced*) and practiced. "Speak the speech, I pray you, as I pronounced it to you, trippingly on the tongue"—over and over. But the words just came out wrong. I sounded like a character from a cartoon. Instead of *pray*, of course I said "pway." And *speech* sounded like "sheets."

In my mind I could hear the raucous laughter of the class. The needling and putdowns were larger than life in my head. *Maybe, if I get really sick that day,* I schemed, *I won't have to read. No, that won't work, 'cause he'll know I'm pretending, and he'll make me read twice as much next week.*

My insecurities worsened as the moment of truth approached. I wanted to leave the country—go anywhere I could be by myself. D-Day came, and I walked to school feeling like a condemned man heading to his execution. *It's now or never,* I thought.

I do believe Mr. Armstrong had a nasty smirk on his round face.

As I trudged into the room, he singled me out with . . . "Good morning, Jerry. I hope you're ready today. I don't expect any mistakes."

As I sat down and the bell rang—like a death knell—my classmates were finding their desks. "Ladies and Gentlemen," the robust teacher announced with fanfare, "this is a very special day. Jerry Dahmen has practiced his reading for several days and should be ready by now."

All my systems were in a state of shock. *Now or never. Now or never. But why now?*

Twenty-three pairs of eyes were riveted on me as Armstrong commanded, "Jerry, it's your turn. Step to the front of the room."

Inch by inch I shuffled to the speaker's stand. I was coming unglued—knees shaking, body pouring perspiration, throat feeling dry as parchment. My voice, if you could call it that, was about to create havoc in the classroom.

As I cautiously turned around to face the class *and* the militant instructor, I took a deep, deep breath. *Now or never . . . Now or never . . .* I stood there transfixed.

"Jerry," Mr. Armstrong snapped, "give us the reading now. We don't have all day. Get on with it!" Several kids were stifling their snickers. I glanced at the paper in front of me. Then . . . another deep, deep breath.

> Speak the s-sheets, I pway you,
> as I pwonounced it to you,
> Twippingly on the tongg"
> (delivered in a high and
> squeaky voice) . . .

Bedlam broke loose as the kids roared. I was praying for a sudden disappearing act.

"Before you do more destruction to *Hamlet*," Mr. Armstrong sharply chided, "please shut up. If you utter so much as one more word, Mr. Dahmen, Shakespeare will roll over in his grave. Sit down right now before you damage that voice of yours even more!"

Gales of laughter and a steady barrage of verbal darts punctured me as I bolted for my chair. "Sit down, little boy!" "Go home to mummy, baby!"

I was oblivious to the class for the rest of the hour. My only memory is of being "saved by the bell" when it rang. I was the first kid out of the classroom door—and the first out of the building. As was often the case, I ran all the way home.

I had a long, drawn-out crying session. Finally pulling myself together, I vowed to myself, *I will be a public speaker and a radio announcer someday!* How would I ever pull myself out of the mental gutter and make that happen?

First, I had to quit feeling sorry for myself. The "poor-me" syndrome was a cop-out. What I needed was guidance and expert advice. The school's personnel, such as Mr. Armstrong, weren't concerned about my problem. But someone somewhere was meant to help me.

I am not sure what prompted me to grab the telephone book and search for a speech therapist. But I have a strong feeling there was a bit of Divine support in my quest. I frantically called each therapist (believe me, there were not that many speech therapists in the Sioux Falls directory!).

"If you have a speech problem, I'm sure you'll find adequate assistance within the school system." That was the typical response I received after sharing my plight with them. They did not seem to understand the brick walls I had run against. In desperation, I made one last call. The therapist was identified in the phone book as "Mary Patterson, Speech Therapist, Sioux Falls College."

After several rings, a distinct, warm voice answered, "This is Mary Patterson. May I help you?"

"Yes, you can!" And I explained my dilemma to her in detail. "Please," I implored, "everyone has turned me down, and I need help!"

"No promises or anything like that, but let's get together at my office next Saturday morning at 8."

Bravo! I felt hope for the first time in years. *A college professor is going to meet with me. Maybe she will take me under her wing.*

On Saturday morning I walked (actually ran) from my home several miles away. I arrived early and waited impatiently for Mrs. Patterson outside her office on the top floor of Jordan Hall. At eight, I heard the steps creaking. A voice called out, "Jerry, this is Mrs. Patterson. Are you up there?"

In the best voice I could muster, I sputtered, "I've been here for a while, Mrs. Patterson."

When she reached the top floor, she firmly shook my hand and ushered me into her office. "Listen, Jerry," she explained, "I have a lot of responsibilities at home and here at the college. I don't normally accept private students. But I heard something in your voice when we talked on the phone. You really want to become a good speaker, don't you? If you're willing to work hard, nothing can stop you."

Her words were soothing music to my ears. She was offering encouragement and hope. "But," she warned, "it won't be easy. You'll have to work harder than you ever have in the past. I'll give you assignments, and it's up to you to accomplish them."

That's exactly what I wanted and needed! I thanked her profusely. "Just be here every Saturday morning at 8 AM, and we'll make you the best speaker you can possibly be. That's my promise."

Thus began a pilgrimage of several years. Every Saturday I practiced reading poetry, books, and newspapers, but that was only part of the work cut out for me. I carried material back home and religiously worked every day after school, reading and rereading everything I could get my hands on.

Results were slow in coming, and the daily assignments were tedious. But Mrs. Patterson kept encouraging me. "Your vowels are improving, Jerry." "I think your voice is getting much stronger." "You have more confidence as you read." She kept praising me.

She gave me more than therapy lessons. She taught me about an ingredient I hadn't heard much about until then—self-esteem. She trained me to believe in myself and not to run away from any problems (she always called them "challenges").

Within a few years, I was entering speech contests and actually winning my share of them. I stopped running scared! I thank God for Mary Patterson and her commitment to me. She helped forge my dream into reality.

Maybe that's why the concept of "I Love Life" has saturated my being. People helping others to overcome insurmountable odds must come within each of us. It cannot be mandated by an educational institution or by a social agency. Encouragement isn't a commodity but a quality that must be cultivated in our hearts and spirits.

Although I have not talked with Mrs. Patterson in several years, I think of her often. I have not forgotten the hundreds of hours she unselfishly sacrificed for a kid with a dream. Her commitment to my dream was the inspiration for this story.

Maybe a confused and desperate youngster will someday enter your life. Instead of turning away, try encouraging that youth to pursue his or her dreams. I promise you this: that young person will never forget you. Although you will not expect it, one day that person just might write a story about you!

2
Hope:
My Son Jeremy

"Jeremy doesn't view himself as I did myself . . . He can overlook his size because he has a self-image as a child that took me decades to build."

Jeremy Dahmen

Photo by Robert Sneed

Linda, the boys, and I arrived early at the Vanderbilt University Medical Center. This was our son Jeremy's big day. After years of tests and hospitalizations, Jeremy was being injected with his first growth hormone shot. Back in South Dakota two years earlier, the doctors and medical specialists had stressed repeatedly, "There's nothing we can do. The tests don't give us any indication of what's wrong with your son. You'll have to accept the fact that he's growing very slowly."

"But isn't there any place we can take him where they can find out what to do?" Linda and I asked the pediatrician and endocrinologists.

"Sure," one of them answered, "there's a place in Minnesota that can give him more tests. But I seriously doubt they'll find out anything more than we already know."

Linda and I resigned ourselves to the dismal predictions. If there was nothing that could be done to help Jeremy grow at a normal rate, we decided not to make an issue of it again.

Several years later the tests stopped, and the doctor's appointments dwindled. WSM Radio in Nashville called and asked me to meet with them for a job interview. At that time the most remote thought in my mind was finding help for Jeremy's growth disorder. Linda and I had virtually stopped talking about it. If there was nothing that could be done about his condition, there was no reason to dispute expert medical advice. We found out later that was a mistake.

A month after the interview, when I was offered the position of news director, Linda and I decided the change would be best for all of us. I accepted and moved the family to Nashville, a move that was about to impact Jeremy's life in a way we thought impossible.

When I began my work in Music City, I kept reading about Vanderbilt University's Medical Center. I had heard Vanderbilt had some of the best medical research programs in the world, but I still didn't relate our son's disorder to the medical center. After all, Linda and I were still convinced there was nothing that could be done.

As I was going through my mail one Monday morning, there was a bulky packet of information from the Medical Center. I glanced over the contents and noticed a piece written about the Endocrinology Research Department's special projects for "growth-deficient children." Deep in my often-disappointed mind, a tiny spark of hope was ignited. *What if,* I thought, *those people at Vanderbilt can make our son grow better?*

Instead of throwing away the material, I called Linda at home at once. "Can you believe it? Vanderbilt has some kind of program for kids who aren't growing normally. What do you think? Should we throw caution to the winds and give it another try?"

"Let's do it!" she answered with a lilt in her voice. "If there's one ounce of hope, we'd be denying Jeremy an opportunity if we don't try."

I immediately called the Endocrinology Research Department and nervously inquired of the woman on the other end of the line, "Are you taking any more patients?"

She answered yes. The word had seldom sounded so beautiful to my ears. The only stipulation was that Jeremy would have to be referred by our family physician.

"Nothing to it. I'll call him right away," I replied. I found a pediatrician within a matter of minutes and set up an appointment. After the examination several days later, the pediatrician gave the OK for Jeremy to go to Vanderbilt.

One of the first steps was a three-day stay at the Medical Center Research wing. Before he was accepted into the project, Jeremy underwent extensive blood tests—every twenty minutes for twenty-four hours.

"But, Mommy, do I have to stay in the hospital again? I just don't want them to stick any more needles into me," Jeremy begged. Although he had already been through his share of tests, blood samples, and hospital beds, Linda and I convinced Jeremy we were on his side, and that this time the tests might cause him to grow.

Several weeks after the tests, Dr. Jennifer Najjar of the endocrinology staff called to report the good news: "Jeremy will get the growth hormone shots. He appears to have a shortage of growth hormone, so the shots might stimulate his system. There's no guarantee we'll have any results, but the drug might possibly provide the hormone needed to make him grow normally. The bad news is . . . it will be a month before we can start the treatment."

Hope! For the first time in years, we were given hope. Hope after years of hearing, "I'm sorry. Nothing can be done for your son." I really despise that word *nothing*. It indicated we had given up, and it solidified the helpless feeling that there would never be a change for the better.

Four weeks later we were sitting in the Medical Center's waiting room. The minutes seemed like hours.

I kept thinking of the years Linda and I desperately wanted Jeremy to develop normally. After his growth started slowing down at the age of two months, we felt it might be a temporary condition, but it wasn't. The dozens of tests and hospital stays left us at square one.

Although Jeremy's size didn't seem to bother him, it affected me. His younger brother was such a contrast. Shooting up like an oak tree with muscles bulging, Jeff was, as one of my friends labeled him, "all boy."

Waitresses in restaurants made me cringe when they would look at Jeremy and comment, "Oh, what a cute boy! How old is he?" When we would answer, they would give us a blank stare and exclaim, "He's awfully small, isn't he?" What really bothered me was a nurse who measured his height during one of his many visits to doctors. "Not very big, is he?" she blurted out as the other patients looked on. "How old is he?" When I told her, she glared at him and virtually shouted, "My, he's really small!"

I probably shouldn't have been that sensitive but maybe I was seeing myself in Jeremy. I simply didn't want him to face all the same kinds of problems I had encountered as a child. I know it's wrong, but my childhood memory tapes would automatically start playing. I would remember how it was when I was his age—being bullied and cut down by other kids made it tough on me. Kids can be awfully unmerciful.

But it wasn't fair to compare my childhood with Jeremy's. He's a happy child, apt to have a smile on his face. He doesn't run himself down around other kids as I did. He doesn't hide from them, even if they're bigger—and right now most of them are. Jeremy likes himself, and he isn't dependent on the approval of his classmates. But my son's condition made me relive and more importantly rethink what happened to me as a kid. At the same time, Jeremy taught me how wrong it is to judge ourselves by society's standards of perfection.

"Daddy, I have a new friend today," he would happily report again and again when he came home from school. "That's great, Jeremy," I'd tell him. But, thinking about the kids I ran into as a child, I would remind Jeremy, "not everyone is going to like you."

Jeremy always answered with a "Who cares?" attitude. "If someone doesn't like me, I have friends who do," he'd reply. "Besides, I like everybody."

He loves people and life. As a father, I was trying to inject his mind with my fears, and he didn't buy that! Jeremy doesn't view himself as I did myself. Sure, he wants to grow, but if he doesn't, it isn't the end of the world. He can overlook his size because he has a self-image as a child that it took me decades to build.

Teachers Who Make a Difference

Although establishing a healthy self-image starts at home, I think the educational system can help make or break a child. Unlike some teachers in my elementary school, Jeremy's instructors are compassionate, warm, and authentic. They don't demean him because of his small size. Jeremy's first-grade teacher, Mrs. Sylvia Simmons, remarked that his size didn't bother him, so why should it bother anyone else?

The majority of today's teachers, I think, know the importance of self-image and attitude. "So what if you're not big and tough?" they'll ask their students. "You can still be a lawyer, engineer, or writer." They don't quench that flame of ambition in a child simply because he or she doesn't fit into some contrived picture of perfection.

Advice for Parents with Small Kids

Approximately one in eight- to ten-thousand children in the school-age population, most of them boys, suffers from a form of growth-hormone deficiency. These kids need our support. Dr. Najjar at Vanderbilt Medical Center says many of them, like Jeremy, are the same size or even shorter than their younger siblings. Thus, other people may treat them as younger than they actually are. People make remarks like, "Isn't he (or she) cute?" or they pat them on the head.

What's needed most of all, according to Dr. Najjar, is parental support. "First, they need to understand that there is no ideal height. Parents should give the child more responsibility at home and should communicate with their schools about the problem. We don't want them feeling inferior about themselves."

But, regardless of what any of us do, smaller children are susceptible to being hassled. Some kids feel powerful when someone is smaller. Some adults have the same beastly attitude. But, as one of Jeremy's teachers puts it, "If size and strength were everything, dinosaurs would still roam the earth. They possessed massive tons of strength, power, and size, but where are they today? The ability to think, to love, to feel—that's what really counts. Don't react to the negative emotions of others. Be yourself. You may never be a superstar quarterback, but you can do thousands of other things that are just as rewarding."

"I Am Somebody!"

When I spoke to a fourth-grade class in a rural Tennessee elementary school, I noticed a short poem hanging on the wall. I wish it had been on the wall of my class when I was a kid:
It goes:

> You're Somebody.
> You may be small or tall,

> But you're still important.
> Whether you're fat or skinny,
> That doesn't matter.
> You're Somebody.

I love that poem. If the kids in that classroom are learning about self-esteem and accepting others as they are, they are headed in the right direction.

During my talk, I asked them how they felt about other people being different—in size, shape, and even color.

"No, it doesn't make any difference to me," a blond-headed girl perkily replied. "I like kids for what they are, not how they look."

One of her classmates, a freckle-faced boy with a contagious smile, added, "I know a girl who doesn't have any legs, and she's a neat person." Still another youngster confided, "My cousin is retarded, but we play together, and I like him a whole lot."

Our culture is changing, or at least it is in many classrooms across the country. When we can instruct our children on self-image, self-esteem, and feelings—not only football or being number one in math—we can reach them and make care, compassion, and hope a part of their emotional vocabulary that will be with them for a lifetime.

Super Isn't Always Best

Most parents want super—"perfect"—kids. Good looking, intelligent, popular. With anything less than the Madison Avenue portrayal of what a child should be or look like, some parents feel cheated.

"Why do I have a deformed child?" a father implores. "What did I do to deserve this?"

The question may be unnerving, but if you doubt its validity, all you have to do is check out institutions around the country. Thousands of beautiful kids are disabled. They're waiting for someone to adopt them and make them feel wanted, cared for, and loved. The parents of these children didn't know how to cope with their far-from-perfect offspring.

Fortunately, there are parents who won't give up on their kids —regardless of how serious their physical or mental condition is. Many times the dad and mom believe in the child infinitely more than any specialist.

3
Joy:
Bandy and Laura Wenning

"I just love her so much . . . She's the greatest joy in my life. I'm just so proud of her."

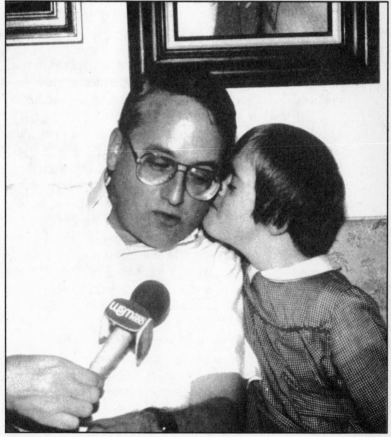

Bandy and Laura Wenning

Photo by David Scarlett

When I pass by the supermarket checkout counter, the headlines of the tabloids always grab my attention. As usual, the covers are dominated by celebrities who are either excitedly expecting their first baby or gushing over one as they leave the hospital.

We are in another baby-boom generation, and many young fathers and mothers are discovering an ingredient that was missing in their lives—a baby—and the joy it brings to them. That sounds syrupy to some people, but ask most couples who have just left the delivery room. Even the "macho" man melts like butter when he holds his child for the first time. Everything about the baby is a miracle—its tiny feet and hands, smooth skin, innocent eyes. A baby has genuine charisma.

A friend of mine, tough on the outside, was a pussycat as he told me about his firstborn. "His soft, little eyes mesmerize me everytime I hold him. I've never in my life been so emotionally touched. What can I tell you? A baby was God's gift to us!"

During a luncheon, a young woman was sitting next to me. She was consumed with excitement since she was expecting her first child. "I'm in public relations and love my work. But something was lacking in our marriage. Things are different now. Now that I'm pregnant, everyone around me in the office wants to have a baby. It's like maybe a child fills a void in our existence."

As a father of three boys including a newborn, Aaron, I know what a child can give a parent. But there is also a risk that's tough to think about. "What if," one of my friends back in South Dakota asked, "my wife and I don't have a healthy baby? I'm not saying we won't take care of him, but I just have no idea how it's going to affect me."

Many prospective parents pose the same question. "Sure, we all want babies who are wrapped in a blanket and are as adorable as a TV commercial for diapers," a social services worker observed. "But there are thousands of couples who aren't prepared for a child who isn't perfect. They're the kids I see every day in our institutions. Parents drop them off and let someone take them off their hands. It's a polite way of saying, 'We can't deal with this imperfect gift from God.' "

Many of these imperfect babies grow up as unwanted young-sters and then become hateful, antisocial adults. "No one ever wanted me as a baby," a seventeen-year-old disabled girl confessed to one of her foster parents. (She had already been placed in over forty homes!) "I'm no good," she cried, "and don't have no love. Never learned how to love."

Unfortunately, too many parents are anxious to give up a child if he/she is "abnormal." And sometimes it's not totally the fault of the couple. Not long ago, some doctors actually encouraged young parents to walk away from the hospital and let the state take charge of a non-perfect baby. They've even been labeled as "throwaway babies."

In his touching book, *One Miracle at a Time,* Irving Dickman, father of a disabled child, wrote:

> Until not too long ago, infants with Down's Syndrome in particular were treated as "throwaway babies." . . . The mother of a Down's Syndrome child was warned not to become "attached to the little vegetable."

One obstetrician, according to Dickman, ordered the parents of a Down's Syndrome baby to "put him away and tell your friends he died."

What a horrible jolt for parents to hear that kind of coldhearted garbage from an authority figure! Would a young couple have the strength and courage to buck the system and take a chance on their baby? I had no idea until I did my homework.

After contacting Janet Jernigan of Outlook Nashville, an agen-cy that provides training services for multiple-handicapped chil-dren and adults, I heard some startling news. "Is this Irving Dickman way off base when he writes these horror stories about 'throwaway' babies?" I wanted to know.

"Unfortunately, what he says is sometimes true," she acknowl-edged. "As a matter of fact, I know of one family in particular that had an experience similar to the one you mentioned, but the couple wouldn't follow the doctor's advice."

Janet put me in touch with Bandy and Donna Wenning and

their fourteen-year-old daughter Laura. When I met them several days later, Laura had her arms wrapped tightly around Bandy's neck. The two were laughing and in an affectionate mood. As Laura kissed and embraced Bandy, tears of joy flowed down his cheeks.

"I just love her so much," the teary-eyed father exclaimed. "She's the greatest joy in my life. I'm just so proud of her!" I was beginning to cry as I watched them.

"C'mon, Laura, can you give me the biggest hug ever?" She wasted no time in responding. Joy isn't in short supply at the Wenning household.

Visiting with them made me both happy and sad—happy because of the strong bond of love between a Down's Syndrome girl and parents who accepted her as she was. But I also sensed sadness because of what the outcome could have been.

"Your Child Will Not Amount to Anything!"

On April 22, 1974, Bandy and his wife Donna were excited. Their firstborn was about to enter the world. They had envisioned this moment for years.

Every minute detail of preparation was thrilling. They picked out baby clothes, fixed up the nursery, and bantered about names for the baby. This was a magic moment . . . but their great expectations would soon be ripped to shreds.

After the delivery, the doctor gloomily announced, "Mr. and Mrs. Wenning, your daughter has Down's Syndrome."

Bandy naively asked, "So what? I've never heard of that before."

"Mr. Wenning, Down's Syndrome is a form of mental retardation that is irreversible." In an unemotional manner, the doctor proceeded to suggest what the Wennings might do.

"Your child will not amount to anything. I believe you ought to have her institutionalized. In my opinion, I doubt if she will live to be six years old."

By now the bad news had sunk in, leaving the Wennings emotionally numb. The cute little outfits, the new fixtures in the nursery at home, even the carefully selected name were no longer important. For the next two or three days the Wennings stayed together and tried to comfort each other. The tears—and the constant questions—kept pouring.

What are we supposed to do? they kept inquiring of their consciences. *Should we go along with the doctor and forget about our baby?*

After the shock of the doctor's suggestion had worn off, and in Bandy's own words, "We stopped feeling sorry for ourselves," Donna and Bandy made a decision: "Our daughter will not stay in the hospital or be sent to an institution. She's our little baby, and we love her," Bandy explained to the doctor. "No one will take her away from us. We won't allow that to take place."

So the Wennings carried Laura home. Even though she didn't understand, they kept telling her, "We're going to be by your side, Laura. No one will take you away from us. We love you!"

The Wennings have made good on their promise. They found help for their Down's Syndrome child. When she was three months old, they began taking her to the Kennedy Center at Vanderbilt University. Over a period of years the staff concentrated on Laura's motor abilities and word/speech recognition. "We'll prove to the doctors you can be an achiever," Bandy constantly reminded Laura.

After the Kennedy Center, the Wennings placed Laura with Outlook Nashville where she continued to progress. Then, she entered the Nashville public school system.

Laura kept on growing and learning. She didn't die by the age of six as the doctor had predicted. The bright-eyed little girl was too busy in school. Although she is mentally disabled, Laura was taught to lip read and recognize colors. She was also able to correspond with a high level of sign language. But that was nothing compared to what Bandy calls . . . "Laura's Miracle."

Don't Say No to Laura

When she was a child, it was necessary for Laura to have a hip replacement. The surgeon was afraid she might never be able to walk. "It was another struggle Donna and I had to face," Bandy confided. "We had to accept that as a possibility. But we sure didn't want to."

Apparently, no one told Laura she wouldn't be able to walk. When she was ten years old, the mislabeled "throwaway" baby slowly, but confidently, took her first steps. "Donna and I cried and thanked God for another miracle," Bandy exulted. "We stayed with our daughter, and so did He. We've worked hard, and so has Laura. And we've been blessed along the way."

"I can't tell you how happy we are," he proudly says. "After all, that kind of medical negativism made it tough on us."

When other parents with handicapped children hear about the Wennings, they seek them out. Their stories, Bandy confirms, are identical. So is his counsel. "I tell them, 'The choice is yours. You can accept the medical prognosis, or you can go with what your heart tells you. Sure, your child might not be normal, but so what?' Laura has been worth our every effort. The joy that comes back to us is our payoff. Yes, we had our doubts at first. Donna and I had a lot of problems when Laura was born. She wasn't working, and I was. We were up most of the night. I'd say to myself, 'I don't know if I can keep on doing this.' But we did, and everything has worked out."

As he talked Bandy's voice was becoming softer. His face was red, and his eyes were overflowing with teardrops. Laura was kissing him and asking for "sugar" from her dad. Even a tough-skinned newsman could not ignore their emotions.

"Everything she has done," Bandy continued, "is first an obstacle and then a proud plateau once she reaches it. For a parent with a normal child, it would seem like nothing, but to a parent with a child who does not make progress very quickly, any stride is wonderful. Laura may never be an average student, but she will be able to express herself, tell you what she wants, and help you get it."

As he hugged Laura, Bandy inquired: "Do you know what my little girl has done for me? She's taught me so much about disabled people. Before she came along, I felt uncomfortable around them.

They even bothered me, but not anymore. At one time I was no different from the doctor who advised us to forget her. He didn't know anything about overcoming handicaps. He gave an opinion that has proven wrong. He didn't talk from knowledge but from prejudiced feelings."

The Wennings never gave up. They refused to relinquish their parental duties—and rights. "We want our baby," they insisted, and they kept her.

After the delivery the couple never saw that doctor again. He is only a memory the couple carries with them. In a way, it's too bad the medical practitioner didn't stay in touch with the Wennings. He might have learned some priceless lessons. Perhaps he has forgotten about the Wennings and their throwaway baby. If only that doctor could have sat in on the interview with us, he might have begun to understand the power of hope and its accompanying joy.

"I don't care what kind of problem it is," Bandy emphasized. "It could be emotional, mental, or physical—maybe all three—but from these years of experience I have found that a handicap isn't a handicap until you make it one. It's our job as parents to give them hope, and sometimes we're the only ones who can."

You'll probably never see the Wennings on the cover of a supermarket tabloid. That's a shame. Although they're not celebrities, the couple has an immense reservoir of goodwill to offer parents who are caught off guard by an imperfect child and even a doctor who seems to extend nothing but gloom and doom.

Knowing the Wennings is to experience ecstatic joy!

4
Perseverance:
Nancy McDaniel

"I do not do it for me, but for the handicapped. The handicapped can do a job if you give them a chance. I know—I handicapped."

Nancy McDaniel (center) with Rebecca Bates (left) and Michelle Smith, teacher

Photo by Lonnie McNorrill

Not long ago I spoke about my childhood experiences at a banquet of volunteer workers. An attractive business woman introduced herself to me after the program and confessed, "I just want you to know that I was hassled as a child. Just like you said—we can grow up, but those memories never leave us and sometimes hold us back from reaching our potential."

Before leaving she wrote a name on her business card and handed it to me. "Please give this young woman a call. If you ever publish the *I Love Life* book, she'd be a terrific story. This person is like us—put down and ridiculed as a child, but she has persevered through the tough times and succeeded far beyond anyone's imagination."

"Nancy McDaniel" was the name of the woman I was to contact. I made the call when I got home. "May I speak with Nancy McDaniel?" I inquired. The person on the other end was Gayle Feltner, director of Duncanwood Day Care Center and School.

As Gayle and I discussed Nancy, I became convinced that Nancy had to be in the book. "Nancy's mental limitations," Gayle exclaimed, "didn't stop her from doing something with her life. You must meet her."

Nancy called me the next morning. *"I'd like to be interviewed, if you promise me one thing. Please call me mentally handicapped, not retarded. Ever since I small, I called 'mentally retarded.' I heard it so many times when I little, I insulted." I gave her my word—and have stuck to it.

"Please Give Me a Chance!"

Nancy was the last of ten children born to hardworking parents who farm in McLeansboro, Illinois. It is thought a lack of oxygen during her birth caused her condition, creating a rough childhood for her. When she was in elementary school at McLeansboro, she found out about acceptance the hard way. Kids poked fun at her because of her hesitant speech, along with her inability to pronounce and articulate her words distinctly.

"They stayed away from me because I didn't talk like them,"

she sadly recalled. "I stuttered and couldn't talk right. I so ashamed of myself."

As Nancy verbalized her painful memories, I remembered the ribbing given me back in South Dakota. But Nancy and I have a point in common: neither one of us was willing to take a back seat to anyone. She was determined to stand up for herself. When she was fourteen years old, the pretty, perky girl enrolled in Bowen Center for the Mentally Handicapped in Harrisburg, Illinois, a residence program for children. That gave her a new lease on life.

"I learn so much there and able to speak a lot better than before. I also got so many skills that help me get work later on," Nancy proudly reported. There she was introduced to the Special Olympics. Nancy remained at the Bowen Center until she was eighteen years of age. After that, the confident young woman returned to her hometown, where she worked for three years as a nurse's aide at the Hamilton Memorial Nursing Home. But Nancy had a dream that would not fade away. She wanted to move to Nashville and work with handicapped children.

"That's crazy," some of her friends advised her. "You'll be disappointed if you try to find work and fail. Stay where you are." Nancy wasn't swayed. She realized her disability could hurt her chances of landing work in Nashville. She couldn't read and wouldn't be able to pass a driver's license test. If she moved to Nashville, she would have to stay with her sister and depend on the family for transportation. *So what?* she thought to herself. *I want to find a job with handicapped kids so I can help.* Nancy made the move!

Finding work in Nashville, she discovered right away, wasn't going to be a snap. Wherever she went, the answer was the same: "You're handicapped. We just can't hire you. What can you do?" Nancy pleaded with potential employers, "I'll wash the children, pick up laundry, get ice water. I want to work so bad. Please—give me a chance!"

For a long time her pleas were unheard. But Nancy was already accustomed to being turned down. She had lived with rejection before. She wasn't about to climb onto a bus and head back to Illinois.

"No one want me because they said I retarded and could not do a good job, but I did not leave the city. I made up my mind to find a job here." Nancy burned that goal into her heart and mind, and it was about to become a reality. She kept a smile on her face and an extra pair of shoes handy, just in case the ones she had wore out from the miles of walking to and from job interviews. When she least expected a response, Nancy's perseverance was about to deliver the goods.

"One day, when I so tired from going to see people, I sitting home and got a call from Duncanwood School. I couldn't believe Gayle, the director, when she tell me, 'Nancy, you're hired.' " Nancy's face was beaming as she recalled the experience. It was her accomplishment, and she wanted that to be her message—people with disabilities can be as persevering as anyone else. The best aspect of her job is how much she loves the work—changing diapers, feeding the children, and doing whatever she is asked to do. But there is another angle to her work that is not written into the job description. Nancy is helping little children conquer the same problems she has overcome.

Speaking with clarity and sincerity, Nancy celebrates her work. "I love the little ones. I want to tell them how much they can accomplish. Even though they disabled, there lots of things they can do."

Nancy doesn't merely talk about what she wants to do. She does it! Since moving to Nashville, she has served as president of People First of Tennessee, a self-help advocacy group for physically and mentally handicapped individuals. She has passionately spoken on the steps of the State Capitol during rallies for the mentally disabled. With her voice trembling and her eyes brimming with joyful tears, Nancy communicates from the heart: "Give us the chance . . . we are human and need to be heard!"

But Nancy's lobbying activities have not diverted her attention from the Special Olympics. When she's not giving speeches, attending legislative hearings, and working at Duncanwood, Nancy slips into her jogging outfit and participates in road races. She even won a bronze medal in the fifty-yard dash during the 1986 United Kingdom Special Olympics Summer Games in England.

An Unforgettable Call

When she flew back to Nashville after the Olympics, Nancy was called to the phone at work. "It's a long-distance call, Nancy," she was informed. "I think it's someone from Washington, D.C."

"Nancy, this is Eunice Kennedy Shriver," the caller calmly explained. "You're one of eight people, including three physicians, to receive the 1986 Kennedy International Award for outstanding contributions in the field of mental retardation. Congratulations!"

Nancy at first thought someone was playing a joke on her. But the more Mrs. Shriver talked about the award, the more Nancy became convinced she wasn't being teased. "But, why me? I not special," she told Mrs. Shriver. "Besides that, I can't come to accept it. I don't have any vacation left."

Mrs. Shriver assured Nancy there would be no problem in getting her to Washington. After all, the awards are equivalent to the Nobel Peace Prize and have been given only six times since 1962. (When she hung up the phone, Gayle told Nancy that extra days would be extended to her. Yes, she must go to D.C.)

A Tribute for Nancy

Nancy will never forget November 17, 1986. She was on stage at the National Academy of Sciences in Washington. Sargeant Shriver hugged her and read a tribute written by former pro football star and sportscaster Frank Gifford. As Shriver read the tribute, Nancy burst into tears before the vast audience. The joy was overwhelming. All the years she suffered, all the doors she knocked on looking for work, all the unnecessary ridicule and teasing—none of those were important anymore. This tribute was her moment!

A few years ago, I wrote a book on courage. I'm sorry I didn't know Nancy McDaniel then, because I would have given her a whole chapter. Courage, in my book, is coming from behind and having the guts to finish.

Nancy has done that and more . . . Nancy speaks out loud and clear for everyone who needs a hand, a good word, a friend. Her life is filled with those qualities that Special Olympics stands for: skill, courage, sharing, and joy.

—Frank Gifford

What an achievement! Nancy had arrived. If only the people who doubted her ability as a child and youth could see her now! Maybe they would learn about a handicapped person's determination to succeed.

The honor could have bloated the egos of some—but not Nancy. She downplays the recognition and accentuates the cause. "I do not do it for me, but for the handicapped. The handicapped can do a job if you give them a chance. I know—I handicapped. I can't read or write, but that not stop me. Other people can do it because I can do it."

Perseverance is her middle name. She kept on knocking even when the doors were closed. Nancy would not take no for an answer. In spite of the odds, she prevailed, and nothing prevented her from realizing her dream. But, with her tenacity to "keep on keeping on," what could?

*(Editor's note: For authenticity, Nancy's dialogue in this chapter has been rendered exactly as she spoke it.)

5
Involvement:
Tom Ritter

"I still remember school days at Hollywood High. After spending eight years at a school for the handicapped, there I was in a setting that was a living terror."

Tom Ritter

Photo by Lonnie McNorrill

When I was born, my mother and I were brain-dead for a minute or two, and my system was damaged somewhat. Apparently, the anesthesiologist didn't give my mother enough oxygen during labor, and her heart stopped beating. Although my parents thought I was a normal baby at first, I just wasn't right. I tilted to one side when I sat up and grabbed objects only with my left hand. Mom's doctor later diagnosed my condition as cerebral palsy. That didn't mean much to me as a child, but the reality of the disorder hit me like a ton of bricks as I grew up.   —Tom Ritter

I was caught off guard as I picked up the telephone. "Mr. Dahmen, this is the President's Committee on the Employment of the Handicapped in Washington. Your 'I Love Life' program has been picked as the only radio show to be honored by the committee this year."

My first reaction was, "You're putting me on." But the woman assured me it was true and gave me her office number if I wanted to verify it. By then I had dropped the phone and was trying to regain my composure. "If I'm the radio winner," I tried to ask calmly, "who are the television winners?"

"You have probably heard of the Ritter brothers from California," the secretary responded. "They are the recipients for the video media." I later found out that John and Tom Ritter had put together a dynamic documentary entitled "Breaking Ground," featuring actors with disabilities. I was astounded to be on the same program that included nationally recognized names. Here I was—a kid from South Dakota who had been told he would never survive speech therapy past the seventh grade—being honored in Washington for a radio show that shouldn't have been successful in the first place, at least according to early feelings of some media people who thought it was crazy and didn't have public appeal.

Naturally, I wanted to learn all I could about the Ritters. (I was already thinking about a possible "I Love Life" interview with them.) I was aware that their father, Tex, who had passed away in 1974, was among the most loved and respected country-and-western singers of all time. I also knew that John Ritter was a successful actor who has starred in several popular TV series over the past few years.

However, I didn't know much about Tom, except that he had been born with cerebral palsy. That prompted me to delve into his background. Although he wasn't a nationally known celebrity, I sensed he had a message that could help others. I later discovered that Tom is a leader in working disabled actors into the media. Merely a list of his achievements was enough to tell me Tom was a "can-do" person. He had attended the University of Southern California, graduated from the University of California (Berkeley), and then earned a law degree from Vanderbilt University in Nashville.

After law school, Tom stayed around Nashville and then decided to follow his dream to Hollywood where he worked in television and movie production. One of his television specials earned him an "Emmy" for the 1985 production of "Superfest," an inspiring production which showcased excerpts from five award-winning documentary and dramatic films that depicted the experience of living with a disability. What a mover! Tom obviously didn't sit around moaning, "I won't be able to go beyond what I have already done."

When the long-awaited day arrived for the awards luncheon, I anxiously flew out of Nashville, accompanied by Opryland Senior Vice-president Tom Griscom, a long-time friend of the Ritters. We were headed for the Washington Hilton, site of the President's National Conference on Handicapped Employment. Over five thousand people, many of them disabled, were converging on the hotel. Most of them were in the main conference room, listening to recognized personalities, including James Brady, special assistant to President Reagan (several years before he had been shot, as was the President, during an attempt on the President's life). Standing next to Brady was Tom Ritter, MC for the gathering. As Tom spoke I could pick up a slight hesitancy in his speech, but he also projected sincerity and eloquence. The more I listened, the more captivated I was. I was now fully convinced he had a story worth hearing.

After the conference I had occasion to observe Tom at the luncheon. With a limp in his left leg, Tom slowly moved to the podium, yet he radiated confidence as he smiled brightly and shook the many outstretched hands.

After the luncheon Tom and I visited about "I Love Life." "Tom, I want you to tell your story so it will relate to people with or without disabilities." That would pose no problem, he assured me, but he would have to wait until he returned to Los Angeles from his honeymoon.

In the meantime, I wanted to discover all I could about him. I had heard that Ralph Emery, host of the popular Nashville Network show, "Nashville Now," had been a dear friend of the late Tex Ritter and his family. Tex and Ralph had been disc jockeys together for a year and a half on WSM Radio in 1966 and 1967. During that time Ralph and the Ritters became close friends.

"Both Tex and his wife Dorothy Fay were very positive people," Ralph mentioned. "Dorothy was a very up person. I always said if I owned a public-relations firm, she'd be the first person I would hire. She gave Tom so much positive reinforcement. I think he was really fortunate to have Dorothy and Tex as parents. They gave him a lot of love and encouragement, and because of Tom, the two became heavily involved in United Cerebral Palsy campaigns to help raise money for other people who have the disorder."

While I was writing this chapter on Tom, his mother was recovering from a stroke at her California home. Both Tom and John inherited their mother's determination to live every day to the fullest.

"She was the rock in the family. Back when Tom was just a little boy, and Tex was on the road a whole lot, Dorothy fulfilled the role of both parents," Ralph observed. "She's always been there for him. She had a great attitude. I don't think she ever had a gloomy thought. That continued after Tex died, and there were some hard financial times for the Ritters. Dorothy remained positive and full of humor, and that obviously was passed along to her sons.

"I still think about the time," Ralph remembered, "when she had Tom and John running errands and taking Christmas packages to her friends. Again they were doing it together, something Dorothy felt strongly about in treating Tom normally.

"A funny line came out of all this. Dorothy didn't cook. All their meals were eaten out. I don't even think they had a kitchen. So, there she was at home wrapping presents, and as the boys were ready to make their deliveries, she told them, 'By the way, if you stop at anybody's house, and they're having a party, would you pick up a few sandwiches and bring them home to your Mom?' John instantly replied, 'What should I ask for—a *mother bag*?' "

Tom Ritter's Triumph Over Cerebral Palsy

All my contacts with Tom confirmed what Ralph had told me about the Ritter family. Tom really does care about people. He has the credentials to prove it. He has co-produced television specials about the disabled, hosts a radio show, and is active in the United Cerebral Palsy Foundation as a co-host of their annual telethons. It's his way of saying, "Here I am with cerebral palsy. What can I do to make the disability secondary to life?"

Tom feels strongly that, "The key to educating people *without* disabilities is through the media. They need to see the successes of those who are disabled." That's why I have included Tom in this book. He has already achieved personal success and is sharing a message for both the disabled and able-bodied: All of us have to understand what a disabled person goes through before we can understand their needs, their desires, and the pain of their everyday lives.

Feeling like a misfit among other kids as he was growing up, Tom kept his feelings to himself. Even close friends of the family like Ralph Emery never knew. "I had known him for years and never realized how much he felt like an outsider. But he made a speech before an annual Cerebral Palsy Fundraiser and totally caught me by surprise. He told how he had felt like an outsider.

Yet, in our private conversations, it had never come up. It was just the way things were, and nobody made a big deal out of it. It may have grown bigger in Tom's mind than in his parents' minds."

Although he had bottled up his feelings all those years, Tom can't forget how it was growing up with a disability, feeling the teasing and loneliness. "I'm twenty months older than John," he said, "but John really acted as the older brother in protecting me from the neighborhood bullies. It was really difficult for me to associate with many of our able-bodied playmates who didn't know how to treat me unless John or one of our closest buddies interceded and suggested it was OK for me to play with them. So many times, kids would keep their distance from me, not out of malice. Rather, they felt uncomfortable about how to relate to someone who was 'different,' someone with a disability."

As Tom talked, I thought back to the kids in my high school who were shunned because of physical abnormalities. It wasn't right, but—as the saying goes—"kids will be kids." I didn't have a physical disability, but I wasn't a "jock." I projected an image of timidity and insecurity around the other kids. Instead of expressing my feelings, I kept them hidden deep inside. Like Tom, I wasn't willing to stand up and assert myself.

Tom recalled, "I still remember school days at Hollywood High. After spending eight years at a school for the handicapped, I was in a new setting that was a living terror. Talk about feeling alienated! I was all by myself. John hadn't been with me the first year. When I was at the handicapped school, I had been the kingpin because I was the most mobile of all the students. Just the opposite was going on at Hollywood High. I didn't have feelings of bonding like I had with the other disabled kids. I still remember when I tried to play touch football with some of the able-bodied kids. John, some friends, and I were having fun playing in the neighborhood. One fellow, who later became a friend, wouldn't play. He apparently didn't know how to deal with me, using some excuse like having a headache. But all of us kept telling him it was all right to play, and he shouldn't worry about breaking me."

Several years earlier Tom had been pushed around by a bully

who rode his bike into the neighborhood. He started calling Tom, John, and their playmates names. Then he pushed Tom until he fell down. "John and some of my friends started getting on him, but I was embarrassed about the whole thing. As I look back, I will say it did teach me something: You really can't rely on your friends and family to do everything for you. You can depend on them for support, but not for everything."

Tom never did stand alone. His family was always there. "I was blessed in having my parents and brother. They never shunned me. Dad, Mom, and John treated me as though nothing were wrong. Growing up with a famous father meant he was gone a lot. But when he was home it was quality time and he took an active part in parenting. I know some parents want to avoid the issue of disability in their child if he doesn't turn out the way they hoped for. They just don't know how to cope with the situation. I was fortunate since my parents were supportive. They knew my physical activities were limited, but they encouraged me to do the best I could. My parents instilled that in me. 'No matter what situation you face,' Dad used to say, or, 'regardless of what kind of cards you were dealt, you need to play with them and do the best you can, even if you have to bluff.' So that attitude was ingrained in me as a youngster. I also learned that helping other people understand their conditions and how to improve their lives was just as important."

As Tom talked I thought about my son Jeremy and the day his elementary school sponsored a Special Olympics program. "Daddy," he excitedly said the day before the games, "I really want to get a ribbon!"

"But, Son," I cautioned, "some of those other kids are bigger than you. They have longer legs, and they can run faster. Some are stronger and are able to jump higher. Just do the best you can, and Mom and I will be very happy."

When we picked him up from school after the games, Jeremy, with an ear-to-ear smile, raced to the car. "Daddy, Mommy, look—I have a ribbon!" My heart revved up, and I became tearful.

"Jeremy, what did you get that ribbon for?" (It was a big red ribbon and was pinned to his shirt.)

He shouted, "The other guys got first-place medals, but the teacher told me I tried real hard and earned this ribbon. I'm so happy I tried!" Just because Jeremy isn't the same size as the rest of his classmates, that hasn't stopped him from doing the best he can.

It's a fact of life that some people can't or won't accept someone who isn't "normal." They deal with their own insecurities by either ignoring or picking on the individual. Tom Ritter learned how to deal with that kind of ribbing in college. "It's unfortunate there are people who tease others because they are physically different from what our society considers 'normal.' When I'd travel with Dad during his frequent tours in the U.S. and overseas, we'd occasionally bump into someone who didn't know how to handle my disability. Maybe a person would make a wisecrack about me or treat me condescendingly.

"Once, in another country, a gentleman treated me as if I were mentally retarded. I guess a lot of people think if you're physically disabled, you must also be mentally disabled. This man was introducing Dad and me. He remarked to Dad, 'Don't worry, Tex. I'll take care of him.' The fellow 'took care' of me when he announced to the crowd that Tom was 'a little slow.'

"Later, I told Dad this fellow was making me feel uncomfortable. Dad told the man, in a gentle manner, 'Tom has a college education and is with me as part of his vacation. I'm not his attendant, and I don't even have to take care of him because he can take care of himself.' To this day I appreciate Dad standing up for me, instead of letting the guy continue with his preconceived ideas that I was a little slow mentally. Back then, I was shy and didn't confront people like I should have."

Tom was learning to be self-reliant. "I have friends who are quadriplegic and aren't able to do much without the aid of an attendant," Tom pointed out. "But it's up to them to tell the attendant what they need. The attendant isn't a mind reader, and that's a mistake I made. I expected everybody to be my mind reader. I had wanted to attend the University of California at Berkeley. For quite a while I didn't communicate my unhappiness about being enrolled at USC. Through it all I learned you have to be assertive and tell people what you want. You've got to let them know your needs and feelings.

"Because of my disability, I never took advantage of the opportunities my father and brother could have given me. I didn't have any role models or see any people with disabilities in front of a news camera. I proceeded to think of myself as a writer or going to law school. But 'the times are a-changin'.' You do see a lot of people with disabilities in the limelight today, but they haven't depended on their disabilities to make it. That would be saying, 'This person is a certain nationality or color, so we will give him a job to fill a quota.' That isn't going to work, specifically with a disabled person. We still have the major studio heads and network executives who are trying to understand the issue of disability in the social context. Yet, they are still not convinced that a disabled person can do the physical job that someone else can do." But in his capacity as a board member of the Corporation on Disabilities in Telecommunications, a non-profit organization that promotes the integration of the disabled into the media, Tom is doing his utmost to move the mountains of negative opinion.

"I am making this point: You really have to learn your craft and more than just acting. I remember our father telling John, who is able-bodied, of course, 'If you want to be an actor, that's fine, but learn other aspects of it. Learn set design and directing. If you're out of work in one field, you can find work in another.' "

Tom Ritter's role model is Franklin Delano Roosevelt who was elected as President of this nation for an unprecedented four terms. Roosevelt was a disabled person who used a wheelchair. He was handicapped in body but brilliant in mind and spirit. Roosevelt triumphed over polio and is remembered as one of America's great chief executives. His was a constructive life.

That is the desire of Tom Ritter's heart—a caring, constructive life. Because of his contribution to the media and to the cause of fund raising for cerebral palsy research, Tom is letting others know what a disabled person can do. And that is well worth knowing.

6
Praise:
Bob Hardin

"Nothing can assure anyone that natural talent will take you anywhere. . . . If you have the desire, you're going to get there."

Bob Hardin

Photo by David Scarlett

Management experts like Tom Peters, author of *In Search of Excellence,* make big bucks trying to pound business sense into managers. "Being a seminar leader or a boss," he scolds his audiences, "involves being human and sensitive to the people around you. Qualified men and women won't be intimidated or suckered anymore. They'll leave and take their knowledge and skills to a business that sincerely cares about them—not just as employees, but as human beings."

And how can managers demonstrate genuine interest in their employees? *Praise.* It is an absolute necessity in management. Nikki Scott of Universal Press Syndicate was right on target when she wrote:

> It's a simple "thank you" or "well done." No flowery speeches, no phony effusiveness. But slowly the people who work for you begin to care . . . about their work. That kind of caring can't be legislated. No manager can demand it. It comes only when people know their hard work is recognized and appreciated—something too many employees hear too seldom in most offices.

I would love to see this kind of classified ad in the Sunday newspaper:

> *WANTED:* A job manager who is sensitive to his or her employees and has the ability to help them with their needs, goals, and desires.

I've talked with managers at motivational seminars who bubble over with: "This is fantastic stuff. I feel like a million bucks!" But when they return to their offices, the content of the session has become ancient history. They gruffly walk to their offices oblivious of everyone around them.

One secretary sadly confessed: "My boss never paid any attention to me for seven years. He never thanked me for the extra assignments I did for him—and there were tons of them. But if I made one little mistake, he'd blow up like I'd committed a major crime." Instead of putting up with the boss' unwillingness to praise her, she found work at a competing company that wasn't shy about telling her, "Thanks, you did a fantastic job! We're fortunate to have you!" Now, even if she were offered more money and benefits, this once-disenchanted secretary wouldn't even consider thinking about returning.

What Happens When There Is No Praise?

One Saturday morning, my middle son Jeffrey and I went to the supermarket to buy some pastries. It was almost impossible to be waited on, even though the bakery counter was not busy. Finally, after minutes of waiting, I was given a gruff snarl and an icy glare by a young woman, demanding, "All right, whatta ya want?" She literally threw our goodies into a bag and escaped into the backroom.

Before checking out, Jeffrey and I bought a Mother's Day card. I noticed how attractive and well-stocked the card section was.

The cashier at the checkout counter stood as solemn as a bronze statue. Without the slightest acknowledgment of our presence, she snapped, "Where's the price on these rolls?" On the in-house phone, she found out the price, and barked it out loudly.

How I wanted to tell those two employees, "Hey, you don't know what you're missing. You obviously hate everything you're doing. Why not walk out now and do something else? Don't waste your time and energy just existing—start living! Why not give some joy to those around you?"

Maybe the management of that supermarket chain is partly to blame. Some companies are so wrapped up in fancy marketing and promotional schemes that they lose track of what it takes to please the customer—primarily employees who enjoy their work.

Every company should motivate its employees and praise them for what they're doing right. That's not taught in business administration school or printed on year-end expense statements. Praise can come from each one of us. If a manager is willing to go the extra mile and give his employees credit for their work, on-the-job performance and productivity will increase. But if the boss mentions only the mistakes, you don't have to be a Tom Peters to explain the low morale.

They Were "in Sync"

Several days after the supermarket incident, I was watching a class at a martial-arts school. Our older son Jeremy was determined for me to enroll him in one of the children's classes, but I was reluctant, even though the martial arts had captured my attention. Jeremy's size made me anxious about signing him up for lessons. Before deciding, though, I wanted to meet the teachers and find out about the classes.

As I walked into the school, I noticed how warm and friendly the staff and pupils were. The atmosphere was exactly the opposite of the supermarket. After introducing myself to one of the employees, I explained about Jeremy and how badly he wanted to enroll in their school.

"If you don't think your boy is ready," he politely suggested, "talk to the owner before you leave." I figured it was worth the time.

As I waited, I began to sense what was happening at the school. The kids and adults were "in sync" with one another. No one was ordering anyone else around, although the ranking system obviously let the students recognize who was in charge. *If only some of the tough-guy bosses I had known could witness this kind of interaction,* I thought.

As I glanced around, I noticed at the far end of the room a bearded man who appeared to be in his thirties. He was quietly talking with several of the students. His right arm hung loosely from his shoulder. "That's the owner, Bob Hardin," one of the instructors told me.

I introduced myself and pointed out why I was there. "Mr. Hardin, one of my boys wants to join your school. He's very small for his age, and I'm worried that karate may be too rough on him."

"Don't allow his size to be a handicap," he answered quickly. "Your son could be a tremendous martial artist someday, but you'll have to encourage him just as much as any of my instructors would have to. You see, the handicap isn't a problem—it's how we react to it." The more he talked, the more I wanted to find out about his background. That's where this story begins.

Armed with Courage

When he was three years old, Bob Hardin was stricken with polio at his Arkansas home. He was "special" in a way, since he was one of the last children in the nation to contract the disease. Placed in an iron lung, a device for artificial respiration, Bob survived the ordeal. His mother still calls Bob's recovery a miracle.

"If you were put into an iron lung," she later told him, "that was supposed to be the end of your life!" The polio left its mark on his body—a paralyzed arm with only enough strength to hold a piece of paper.

During his childhood, even simple, everyday actions most of us take for granted were tough for a boy with one working arm. That handicap didn't keep him down. Instead, it forced him to be creative. He recalls using the door knob in his bedroom as a quick way to slip on a T-shirt. By stretching the shirt over the knob, he could slide his head through the top and pull on the shirt. Trial-and-error techniques, however, didn't work as well at school. Some of his classmates were skeptical about what he could do.

"I always felt I could do anything, but I seldom had the chance to get them done," Bob remarked. "As a kid I was always the last guy picked on any team. The others misjudged me because of the one bad arm. They didn't think I'd be an asset."

But his paralyzed arm forced him to excel. His handicap inspired him to go beyond what was expected of him. "If given the chance, I've always felt I could achieve."

How does he achieve? "I motivate myself to advance. Nothing can assure anyone that natural talent will take you anywhere. It's the individual who has the guts to go beyond the point where most people throw up their hands in disgust and decide to find something else to do. If you have the desire, you're going to get there!"

Bob was fortunate. As a child, his parents gave him the support system he needed. They were sensitive to his needs but wouldn't let him feel sorry for himself. They offered praise in copious amounts. His mother kept on telling him, "If no one likes you, who cares? Just remember, Son, you can do what you want to do." Those words of encouragement sank in.

Unfortunately, like many employers, there are parents who don't provide positive nurturing. I've heard parents tell their kids in public places, "You drive me nuts! If you don't shut up, I'll knock your stupid head off!"—and worse.

Some managers subtly keep their staff in line by intimidation. "If you make a mistake, it's your job." Is it any wonder why some kids and employees are not motivated?

Praise apparently produces results. Walking around Bob's martial-arts studio and watching his students showed me that. Unlike a high-school class or a job, they didn't have to be there. These students were paying for the privilege, and in return they were learning how to protect themselves—and much more.

I learned to see how much his students respect Bob. Although he is far beyond them in knowledge of the art, Bob doesn't put them down. He bestows praise on them. "I sit down and talk with them," he says. "I tell the ones who have handicaps that most of us don't use all the potential we have anyway. If they train twice as hard with one hand, they're going to have a punch that's stronger and faster than most opponents. When I watch someone making any kind of progress, however minor it is, I'll compliment him in class. He'll never forget it."

Bob's philosophy has worked for him and his school. In a business that has a high attrition rate, the teacher with one paralyzed arm has developed more than five hundred black belts, including several national champions! Bob, incidentally, has already achieved the rank of sixth degree black belt and is considered one of the nation's most powerful martial artists.

Before leaving the studio, I decided to enroll Jeremy in the school. Regardless of how rapidly he developed, I knew he would be with someone who cared about him and his development.

Meeting and knowing Bob reaffirmed the power of praise and the importance of parents, bosses, and teachers to open their hearts and eyes and keep on feeling. If they don't, they can't possibly understand the people around them. These "authority" figures must replace heavy-duty criticism with positive reinforcement at home and at work. Before that can happen, they must become aware of their insensitivity and the irreparable damage it can inflict on other human beings—whether at a seminar, at home, at school, at church, or in business.

Those who think their fears, doubts, and negative feedback aren't affecting someone else aren't being honest with themselves. Parents can build up their children or rip them apart. Employers and teachers can wreak the same havoc on their employees and students. Verbal abuse is no different from physical. In one sense, it is just as degrading and lasts much longer than the bruises and pain of a physical beating.

When he was a youngster, Bob Hardin's mother expressed it well: "Everyone of us in this great, spacious world is special, and we have the right to feel good about ourselves."

Bob never forgot those fortifying words. He has passed them on to each of his students, including my son Jeremy, a small and persistent boy who has earned his blue belt! It has required hard work, practice, and praise from his parents and, of course, from Bob Hardin.

Part II:
Special People

7
Compassion:
The Zemba Family

"With all my heart, I feel this is our calling . . . if I couldn't call on the Lord every night and ten or eleven times during the day, we couldn't make it."

Photo by David Rogers

The Zemba Family (Nadine, fourth from left, second row; Wendolyn, far right, second row)

The "I Love Life" interviews have touched my mind and heart. These are not professional interviewees who spout pat, sterile responses. Rather, these "ordinary" but amazing people, who have beat extraordinary odds, have freely opened their hearts and souls. I've shared hugs, laughter, tears, and prayers with many of them. Since their stories are personally overpowering, I become choked up simply hearing how they have coped with adversity. They make me feel truly human and not separated from genuine feelings.

Certain media people have become caught up in their own game and take themselves too seriously. Somehow they want to isolate themselves completely from any victim. They have become arrogant and are seemingly devoid of emotion. Oftentimes, the victim suffers.

I still become angry when I think about an abrasive young reporter who was covering a fire at a major hotel in the Midwest. He was preparing for a live telecast from the scene for his ten o'clock report. Cued by the cameraman with a hand sign, this brash fellow yelled at the top of his lungs to an elderly lady who was covered with residue from the blaze: "Get over here right now, Lady!"

This terrified woman, on vacation with her husband, had just lost everything in their room. She was suffering from heavy smoke inhalation, and her husband had been rushed to a hospital with severe burns. She didn't even know his condition when he was placed in the ambulance. The reporter's only concern was to put her on the air before anyone else could interview her. With his microphone stuck an inch away from her mouth, he demanded her immediate reaction to the fire. Instead of speaking, she burst into tears. Unable to handle it, he cut short his report and walked away from the distraught woman.

Dr. Roy Peter Clark, one of the nation's best-known writing coaches, spoke at a symposium on "Crime Victims and the Media." Dr. Clark graphically described a nightmare experience during a family vacation.

"We stopped for a night in a motel along the interstate in

Charlotte, North Carolina. The next morning we were robbed by a man with a gun. He threatened to blow my daughter's brains out, herded us into the bathroom, and robbed us of our belongings. Although he never laid a hand on us, he changed our lives forever. There was nothing written or broadcast about the robbery, but I have often wondered how I would have greeted a reporter or photographer at that devastating moment."

Fortunately, we in the news media are finally picking up the message. The Radio-Television News Directors Association is holding workshops and offering information on the handling of trauma victims. It is fully as important, we are learning, to treat the victims with compassion as it is being the first to interview them.

We in the news media must become more human. Look at the medical profession. Many physicians believe that hugs and other forms of openness and compassion are essential to the healing of their patients. Dr. Bernie Siegel, author of the best-seller *Love, Medicine, and Miracles,* treats cancer patients. He also relates to them in a manner that is catching on around the country.

> I . . . stepped out from behind my desk and opened the door to my heart as well as my office . . . I began encouraging my patients to call me by my first name . . . I committed the physician's cardinal sin: I got "involved" with my patients. For the first time I began to understand fully what it's like to live with cancer . . . I began hugging patients.
>
> Later, I found I was saying, "I need to hug you," so I could go on. And even if they were on respirators, my patients reached out to help me with a touch or a kiss. . . . They were saving me.

This has happened to me. The people I have interviewed on "I Love Life" have touched me. But I've allowed it to take place, and I am not afraid of being human.

A Lesson in Compassion

Do you want a real lesson in compassion? Then let me introduce you to the Zembas. The Nashville couple, Nadine and Wendolyn, are a rare breed who have taken in dozens of kids over the years and have adopted many of them. But the story goes beyond parenting. It is about changing the lives of children who are considered "pieces of human garbage" by some.

The Zemba house is anything but spacious or contemporary. There are no expensive rugs or antique furniture. Their home is in an average neighborhood. The porch is loaded with remnants of broken-down wheelchairs. Oftentimes, a passerby can spot a retarded child walking in the back yard. Maybe another youngster in a wheelchair is peering out the living room window. Many people may ignore the house. Some may think it's only another place to put the handicapped.

A visit with the Zembas will leave you feeling far better about people and maybe you'll have tears in your eyes. If you're a parent with a troubled child, you might learn from the encounter.

Divine Persuasion

I had read about the Zembas in a newspaper article. They had been selected as "Foster Parents of the Year" in Davidson County, Tennessee. For nearly three decades they had been in the caring business—but for them it is more than accepting a small check at the end of the month to feed, house, and clothe these children. Nadine and Wendolyn have opened their lives and hearts to them.

The Zembas had reared five children of their own in California. After the kids grew up and left home, the couple felt a void in their lives. "The Lord told us what to do," Nadine declared. "He wanted us to do what we're doing, and He's ironed out the tough spots along the way. With all my heart, I feel this is our calling because we don't have the problems with the kids that other foster parents have had. If I couldn't call upon the Lord every night and ten or eleven times during the day, we couldn't make it."

But it definitely required Divine persuasion before the Zembas filed for their first adoption. "We went home, knelt at the foot of our bed, and prayed for hours. The next day or so I was driving home from work. I had the radio on but wasn't really listening.

All of a sudden, the message sank in. The announcer said, 'There's a lady driving home from work, and the Lord has laid it on her heart to do something she's really concerned about. I have a word for you, Ma'am. The Lord will provide the way for you in what He wants you to fulfill.' "

From that moment on, the Zembas have followed through. There have been minor obstacles, of course, but in every instance Nadine is convinced, "God has been with us all along."

"Why Should Anyone Want Me?"

Mike had been kicked around since birth. Placed in foster homes and institutions since he was nine, the angry youngster hated his mother. She didn't want a son anymore and wanted to get rid of him and her responsibility. Mike was neither retarded nor disabled, but he was not normal, either. Mike had a chip on his shoulder. "Everyone hates me, including my mother. Why should anyone want me?" he would ask social workers who kept finding home after home for him.

I'm not going to stay anywhere very long, he reasoned to himself. And that was the scenario. In a succession of homes, Mike made sure he'd be traded like a used car. The more homes he was in, the less he thought of himself. *No one likes me,* he felt. *Why should I like myself?* Mike's low self-image and self-esteem were deeply etched into his mind.

"We can't handle him," complained the foster parents who kept sending him back to the state. "Well, let's put him over here for a while," the authorities decided. While the bureaucratic channels were checking him in and out of short-term homes, Mike was dying emotionally and had very little feeling. He had built up years of hate and anger and was about to unload everything on his next foster parents, the Zembas.

Mike was sixteen and not about to be pushed around by anyone. The last thing he wanted to hear was another foster family telling him how much they loved him. That turned his stomach. But Nadine didn't stop. "We do want you, Mike," she kept on telling him. "We believe in you. Start to believe in yourself."

He would nod his head in compliance, but Mike was sick of the hugs and kind words. "Just leave me alone and send me away. Everyone else has. What makes you so special?" he angrily asked. Mike wasn't ready for closeness. Labeled a "misfit" and "troublemaker" since he was a child, he wanted to live up to his image as a tough and crazy kid. *I'm going to get kicked out of this place,* he convinced himself. *And I know how to do it.*

The Punch in the Mouth Was Worth It

On a Friday night, the Zembas promised to take Mike and two of his friends to a movie. "Mike was muttering something about this being the night to leave us," Nadine later remembered. "I told him, 'There's nothing you can do to make us send you to another home. We want you here with us.' " But Mike was determined.

He kept following Nadine around the house as she was preparing to leave. All of a sudden, he stood face to face with her. He shouted, "I bet if I hit you right now, you'd send me away."

Nadine looked directly at the angry black-haired teenager. She wasn't about to let him tear down what she and Wendolyn had been building.

"Mike, do you really want to hit me?" she inquired in a gentle tone.

Instantly, as if she had pushed a button, the fury and hate shot out of his dark eyes like electricity. He drew back his left arm and swung at Nadine. The punch landed on her mouth. Blood flew and splattered onto Mike as he stared at the woman who wanted to keep him.

"You're gonna send me away now, aren't you, Lady?" he screamed. "You got to now, don't you?"

"No, Mike, I don't have to send you away, and I don't intend to." Mike couldn't understand her reaction.

As he yelled, Nadine turned and walked into the bathroom. Mike tagged along after her like a puppy dog. "You've got to get rid of me," he ordered Nadine. As she grabbed a towel and dabbed away the blood, unflappable Nadine shocked him with her reply.

"Mike, I have to do something with this mouth, or we won't be able to go to the movie."

"If you don't kick me out, your husband will," he insisted.

"But, Mike, you didn't hit Wendy. That was between us." As she looked in the mirror, Nadine saw her lip sticking out. She tried to clean off the blood, but the swelling got worse. Still not letting the incident worry her, Nadine glanced at Mike and told him, "We've got to get ready to go to the movie."

"You're still taking us there?" the surprised Mike inquired.

"Yes, we planned on the movie, and we're going to see it. OK?"

When they reached the theater, Mike wouldn't talk to Nadine. Instead, he sat behind her. "I could hear the boy nervously wrestling with himself. He was the most miserable kid I've ever seen in my life."

After the movie, Wendolyn drove Nadine and the boys back home. As she was heading to her room, Nadine, who is mechanically minded, told Mike she'd make good on her promise to help him with his car the next morning. "Mike, if you still want me to work on your car, you'd better go to bed. I want to do it early in the morning, because I intend to shop in the afternoon."

Mike followed Nadine to her bedroom and stood by the door. In a subdued voice, he asked, "Are you still going to help me with my car?"

"Why not, Mike?"

"You know," he almost whispered.

"I've already forgotten, Mike."

"But I hit you." Mike paused and stared at the floor. "I'm so sorry." Mike opened his emotional floodgates. The once-angry young man fell into Nadine's arms and wept.

"We had won Mike that one special night," Nadine recalled twenty-eight years later.

Mike stayed with the Zembas and graduated from high school. He left their home and was sent overseas to fight in Vietnam. He returned home and found work in California. Today, Mike is forty-five years old and has a family of his own.

As she reminisces about the night Mike slugged her, the sturdy foster parent becomes sentimental talking about how Mike turned around. With tears in her eyes, she says with pride: "It took a family willing to stick with him, to know he was a good person, and tell him those simple words, 'I love you,' and mean it. And I still say—it was worth the punch in the mouth."

Several months after interviewing Nadine, I was at a regional news broadcasting conference. The gathering included an awards presentation. When the honors were handed out, and the titles of the entries read, one of them plucked my heartstrings.

" 'The Zembas' Invasion,' a story of a family providing a home for disabled children," the MC announced, "has won best feature of the year." A Nashville television station had produced a show about the Zembas and their children.

"That's the kind of news I like to hear," the wife of a broadcaster remarked to me.

"You're right," I answered, "but her story is more than a news feature. It has affected the lives of kids no one wanted."

"You mean, it's not just a happy family taking in little kids."

"No, it's about foster parents who are putting their lives on the line and not giving up, even if they might be punched in the mouth."

I proceeded to tell her about Mike. She left with moist eyes. So did I!

8
Giving:
Mary Catherine Strobel

"'Everybody was her good friend. If somebody did something wrong,' her son Jerry jokingly said, 'her response was, <u>Oh, he had a tough time, but he's good people.</u>'"

Mary Catherine Strobel

Photo Courtesy of the Strobel Family

Who cries for the victims when it's all over?
Where do the beaten kids with broken hearts wind up?
Alone and discarded?
And what about the women, battered and empty?
Where do they hide?
And what about the raped teenager?
Isn't there humanity anymore?

Who's going to care and mend love
when their lives are hanging by threads?

It's the "special people."
The ones who get out of bed at two in the morning
to listen to a wife whose husband just sent her to
the hospital the fourth time
with black eyes and a crushed heart.

And it's "special people" who counsel a young girl,
raped and brutalized.
And what about the battered kids, whose only refuge
is to escape from their parents?

They have "special people" too.

Yes, these people care and love and cry.

They have to.
If they don't, who will?

—J. D.

In the years spent researching "I Love Life," I have interviewed
hundreds of Good Samaritans. They are in every city and town
in this nation, but many go unnoticed as they perform their good
deeds. Most of them do not seek publicity and wish to remain
anonymous.

Mary Catherine Strobel was one of them. She never sought
interviews or recognition during her years of volunteer service in
Nashville. The people who were most aware of her were those she
was trying to help.

Tragically, Mrs. Strobel wasn't news until she was murdered.

The details of her murder initially captured the headlines. As the media dug into her background, we learned she had been an activist for the homeless who did more than merely discuss the problem of homelessness and poverty. She was too busy for talk—she was doing something about those problems on a one-to-one level.

One Person Who Made a Difference

Mrs. Strobel, a beautiful woman in her seventies with snow-white hair, was bursting with the caring, energy, and joy that godly love generated. She had the secret of life at her fingertips—helping others without any guarantee of recompense. She didn't sit around and complain. She was too busy dispelling unhappiness and depression from other people's lives.

"Everybody was her good friend. If someone did something wrong," her son Jerry jokingly said, "her response was, 'Oh, he had a tough time, but he's good people!' If she were present now, Mama would tell you what a great-looking tie you have and how nice your glasses are. Before long, she'd find out everything about your grandmother, and pretty soon she'd delve into your family background and discover you were related to her. She was a beautiful person who found good in everybody and everything."

Mary Catherine Strobel was a doer. The mother of four was always on the go—cooking at soup kitchens, visiting the sick in hospitals—people she didn't know until she dropped by their rooms—even attending funerals, often of the poverty-stricken and disenfranchised (She even kept a spare funeral wreath in her car in case a funeral needed it!). Instead of buying expensive wardrobes, she'd save her money and slip a five- or ten-dollar bill to "a good friend" who was broke—and there were plenty of them.

But she never forgot her family. She taught them Christian values that are inextricably woven into the tapestries of her children's lives. "Mama was always there," Jerry explained. "She had so much energy and was always smiling and laughing. A lot of her love came from her strong faith in God. But she didn't wear her religion on her sleeve. She always said: 'You're not better than anybody, but you're as good as anyone, no matter where they live or how rich they are.' "

Jerry's conversation was laden with respect for a mother who wouldn't turn away from anyone in need. "She couldn't debate the Bible or argue theology. Mama wouldn't and didn't want to do that, but she did believe in feeding the hungry, clothing the naked, visiting the sick and imprisoned, and sheltering the homeless. Mama believed in helping others and spent her life living that way."

Dr. Edward Stainbrook, a nationally known expert on human behavior and contemporary society, must have been thinking about Mary Catherine Strobel's qualities when he told an interviewer several years ago:

> Many people . . . find the future gloomy and feel relatively power-less to shape it. They think that they have no power to influence what is happening to them, so they turn in on themselves and say, "OK, I'll just take care of No. 1." That's narcissism with a vengeance. There must be something beyond self. People must realize that they have a responsibility to someone, to something beyond themselves.

Mary Catherine spiritually understood the power of giving. When she was only nine years old, she asked her father for money to buy food for some needy neighbors. From then on, Mary Catherine never stopped giving.

Whenever I interview a volunteer, I always ask the question: What motivates you to do this kind of work without pay and little, if any, recognition? Each time I always get the same answer in two short, forceful statements: "I have a need inside of me to do it! It makes me feel good!" That is one factor that kept Mary Catherine excited about giving. It was her mission, and she gladly did whatever was required to do the work.

The Newsmaker Who Touched the Soul

Speaking to a luncheon group of several hundred volunteers and community leaders, Jerry Strobel spoke from his heart and soul. In a quiet, but reassuring, voice, Jerry was paying homage to his mother who had been senselessly murdered several months earlier. Her work was being memorialized. The occasion was the first annual "Mary Catherine Strobel Award Luncheon" in recognition of volunteerism.

Mary Catherine's oldest son conveyed his mother's message with confidence and eloquence. He knew, as his mother did, about the power of giving. "Most people in the world today consider service to mankind to be an obligation. A smaller number of people recognize this service to be a privilege. But then there is that group of special people who consider service to mankind neither an obligation nor a privilege. For them it is their very nature, so woven into their being and spirit that they do wonderful work because they can't conceive of doing otherwise.

"Mama's old blue automobile was a rolling general store with supplies of food, clothes, shoes, books, newspapers for paper drives, and other goods for the needy," Jerry softly shared with those at the luncheon. "It wasn't unusual for her to visit the hospitals, assist at a soup kitchen, attend a funeral or two, and take clothing to a poor family, all in the course of what she would describe as a normal day."

To me, the most stirring quote in Jerry's speech was: "Her work wasn't confined to a single religion or to people of one race. My mother's expression after returning thanks for each meal was: 'God bless everybody.' "

What a giver and lover of life! She headed out on her own, her car filled with supplies—but most of all, her heart filled with love that would make others feel better. Mary Catherine wasn't an influential leader in the community. She wasn't on the boards of large charitable organizations. But she was, as Jerry lovingly described her, an "average" person who proved that one human being can definitely make a difference in the world. Mary Catherine gave what she could—not large financial contributions, but her greatest inborn gifts—her time, her good humor, her faith, her love. What a life! What a commitment to mankind!

It's unfortunate that success—at least for many—is calculated in terms of investments, mansions, flashy cars, and yachts. Special people like Mary Catherine are successful from the standpoint of eternal values. Such caring, loving people are fully as appealing and as inspiring as any presidential candidate, socialite, or actor— maybe more so. Mary Catherine never tried (nor did she want) to make pronouncements about the homeless that would be picked up by the media and carried nationwide or even worldwide. Her method was more direct: personal, face to face and heart to heart with another human being.

It is strange how some heroes of our generation are self-destructive. A presidential candidate quits because of an alleged affair and possible sexual misconduct with an attractive woman. In-fighting among television evangelists hurts ministries around the world. Several well-known actors are picked up for assaulting cameramen and attacking pedestrians, and big-name athletes are caught snorting cocaine. What is missing in their lives? They have the money and the independence to do whatever they want—jetting to faraway places, driving costly autos, and living in mammoth homes. But their power, money, and prestige aren't enough to keep them out of deep trouble. They are the "successes" who are idolized and loved by millions.

But a superlative quality was second nature to Mary Catherine Strobel—giving! Instead of flying off to exotic countries, she was hovering over the steam table at a mission for the homeless or stroking the brows of the forgotten sick at a "charity" hospital.

Some perceptive songwriter wrote that it's giving that makes you what you are. When we are taking all the time, life is like a vacuum. We're still empty on the inside, wanting more and more of everything fame and money can obtain for us.

An East Tennessee financier was sentenced to twenty years in prison for money laundering, bank fraud, bankruptcy fraud, and tax fraud. In a letter to the federal judge who sentenced him, C. H. Butcher testified:

> I . . . became obsessed with power and money. This obsession led to the attitude that with enough money and power, I could bypass

or at least outsmart any law or regulation. . . . By coming to terms with the moral issues, I went back to my Christian childhood and remembered the lessons my mother had taught me: a form of success may be obtained by lying and cheating, but the cost in human suffering and moral decay is never worth the price.

Maybe we need to hear and read more about Mary Catherine and the thousands of other volunteers who have fallen in love with giving—men and women who counsel rape victims, go hiking on weekends with boys without fathers, answer telephones until 5 AM at a crisis center listening to callers threatening suicide. Such volunteers bring warmth and love to other human beings. Their work is an incentive to all of us in a world where computerization and depersonalization are slicing away at the fabric of life. We know so much about disc drives and laser beams and so little about our fellow inhabitants on this small planet. Let us not forget the Mary Catherine Strobels who have given hope to the seemingly hopeless around them.

I have no doubt that if God had notified Mary Catherine that she had only twenty-four hours to live, she wouldn't have given thought to her car, clothes, or home. Instead, she would have been at her youngest son's (Charles's) church, making sure that the street people had enough to eat and wear. She expected that of herself and her children. That's what the Strobel family is all about—giving!

You will read about their amazing spirit of forgiveness in the following chapter.

9
A Family's Forgiveness: The Strobel Brothers

"I know some people criticized us for forgiving the killer, but that's our position, and we will stand behind it."

Jerry (left) and Father Charles Strobel

Photo by Brent Stoker

Swept up in the fervor of the Christmas season, our family was preparing to drive 945 miles to South Dakota for the holidays. Hopefully, our boys' Teddy Ruxpin bears might provide enough entertainment to keep them (Jeremy and Jeffrey) from exterminating each other en route. We had also packed enough batteries to last five lifetimes.

As we were about to drive off, Buddy Sadler, our assistant news director, called with shocking news. "Jerry Strobel's mother was found this morning. She had been killed and put in the trunk of her car. The authorities don't know who did it or why." My heart sank dismally within me. As I hung up the phone I immediately thought of Jerry, whom I had known for several months and considered a friend. Whenever I had seen Jerry, he was always teasing and laughing. His sense of humor and positive approach were genuine, down to earth.

Although in top management at the Opry, Jerry is "just folks" and always has time for others. Once I started to find out about his mother, Mary Catherine, I realized where Jerry's beautiful qualities came from.

"We Prayed for Our Mother"

Nashville, Tennessee, December 11, 1986—Mary Catherine Strobel has been missing for several days. After she left the Holy Name Catholic Church, where her son, Charles, serves as the priest, no one except the owner of a beauty shop has seen her, the owner later told police. Mary Catherine had appeared slightly disoriented when she asked for directions to the Union Rescue Mission. Despite a city-wide search for the elderly woman, nothing turned up.

The Strobel brothers, Jerry and Father Charles, decided to conduct a search on their own. They asked a friend, who is a policeman and parishioner in Holy Name Church, to go with them. They backtracked Mrs. Strobel's last-known whereabouts. As they drove in downtown Nashville about 1 AM, the officer suggested they check out the area around the Union Rescue Mission.

"She's probably lost and still alive and well," Jerry and Charles reassured each other. With hope in their hearts, the Strobel brothers and their officer friend drove toward Lower Broadway Street, a tough section close to the Cumberland River. The officer accidentally drove into a one-way street. Realizing his mistake he turned off adjacent to the Greyhound Bus Station. Charles recognized the blue AMC Concord, his mother's car.

They immediately parked the car, walked over to Mrs. Strobel's car, and looked inside. There was no sign of her, so Jerry and Charles decided to open the trunk. Against protests of the police who had arrived on the scene, Jerry sped off to pick up an extra set of keys at his mother's home. When he returned, the officers were reluctant to bother the trunk, but Father Charles pled with them.

As the trunk was cautiously unlocked, they were traumatized. Mrs. Strobel's body was inside. It was soon apparent that she had been strangled and stabbed by her attacker. Father Charles administered last rites, and then the brothers began notifying family members.

"We Forgive You"

The news media converged on the family, wanting instant reactions from the slain woman's children. Instead of granting interviews at first, Charles and Jerry and their sisters, Veronica and Alice, met and wrote out their impressions, and then issued a public statement. Instead of being filled with hate and revenge, the family survivors' statement stressed forgiveness. "After all," as Charles later emphasized, "that's what Mama would have wanted us to do."

The Strobels wrote:

This terrible event in our lives points out how heartless our world can be. But our mother gave us lessons every day about what gentleness and kindness can mean in even the most forgotten lives. No horror can change our belief that the concern and love our mother meant to us and to so many others is the best response to the violence we see all around us in the world.

. . . If this community can be reminded of that and can renew itself to a concern for the troubled and distressed, then we know our mother would smile.

About five weeks after the murder, Texas authorities reported that "Mary Catherine Strobel's alleged murderer has been picked up." William Scott Day had admitted to her murder and five others in a five-week, five-state slaying spree after his escape December 4, 1986, from a Michigan psychiatric institution (the very day he was to be returned to Jackson State Prison) and ended with his capture at a traffic stop in West Texas on January 12, 1987.

Almost immediately the Strobel family was besieged with phone calls from the media wanting interviews with the family. Once again Mrs. Strobel's children issued a statement of Christian compassion and forgiveness.

> The cruelty of her death, as devastating as it is, does not diminish our belief that God's forgiveness and love, as our mother showed us, is the only response to the violence we know. If the suspect is guilty as alleged, it is clear to us that he is deeply troubled and needs all the compassion our society can offer.

"We Forgive You"

What would you do if someone hurt or, God forbid, killed one of your family members? The Strobels had to answer that gut-wrenching question. In their wildest imagination they had no idea someone would snuff out the life of their mother—a woman of goodness and kindness. She was killed while helping the homeless and disenfranchised, which was part of her life.

Where did they receive the power to forgive? Did it work for them? Did they unconsciously harbor malice toward their mother's murderer?

Several months after the tragedy, Charles and Jerry agreed to talk with me about how they were able to survive the experience without loathing the man who slew their dear mother. Although the interviews with Jerry and Charles were not conducted together, their answers were almost identical.

Two Testaments of Forgiveness

Father Charles Strobel began our conversation with: "It's important to express my feelings. Perhaps the families of other crime victims can relate in a positive way to what our family has done." Even though he was dressed in clerical garb, Charles looked boyish with a warm smile and youthful appearance.

Was there ever a time he wanted revenge? "It's a terrible, terrible loss and sadness—but I didn't dwell on who killed her other than thinking whoever had taken her life wasn't right inside. At the same time I just couldn't imagine anyone doing that to her, knowing who she was.

"As everything else began to sink in," Father Strobel continued, his face now somber, "I remember thinking about this person and having the need to say to him, 'We forgive you.' Whether that person needs to hear that or wants to hear it is another thing."

On the other hand, Jerry answered, "I really haven't given much thought at all to the murderer. Somehow, it's like he doesn't even exist. . . . If you lose your mother in a car wreck or she has a heart attack—whatever the reason—it doesn't make any difference. There is pain in the loss of a loved one. In our situation, I just hope and pray Mama didn't suffer."

As Charles and Jerry later found out from the accused murderer's confession, Mrs. Strobel did suffer considerably. Jerry went on: "I do know the person who did this is obviously very sick. Killing is an unnatural thing to do. Unless an animal is starving, it doesn't even kill its own species. The man who took our mother's life was doing something unnatural. She wasn't a threat to him. He had what he needed, some thirty dollars in cash from her and a car to get him out of town—but that wasn't enough for him. I have to think there was something emotionally and mentally wrong with him."

As I interviewed Jerry I marveled at the grace which flowed through him. "If you're a Christian," he emphasized, "you have to practice what Christ said: 'Father, forgive them, for they know not what they do.' You have to believe that an individual doesn't know what he's doing when a life is taken. And then you have to look at the victim's life and hope some good will come out of it."

As I listened to the brothers speak of Christian forgiveness, I also thought of other people's reactions to the murder. A typical comment was, "If anyone ever laid a hand on my family—my mother or father, my kids or my wife—I wouldn't stop until I made them suffer." But Mary Catherine Strobel had reared her four children to follow the path of the Nazarene.

Father Charles clung to the lessons of Christian charity his mother taught him. "During the funeral mass (which he conducted) I said anger and revenge are not compatible with our mother's beliefs. As we all know, there is nothing to be gained if the score is evened. It wouldn't bring back our mother or ease our pain. Just the opposite would happen. Everything would become more difficult, and we in turn would become the extensions of the evil that took our mother."

Awe and wonder are words which aptly describe my emotions as I interviewed the Strobel brothers on more than one occasion.

Father Charles made it plain that forgiveness is an act of the will and that each person has the power to choose. Freedom and peace, Father Charles testified, spring from the choice to forgive. Even though feelings of bitterness and revenge might foment because of wrongs done to us or to our loved ones, those emotions do not come from the will, but rather from being victimized, he explained.

"Unless the victimized person tries to seize control of that with God's help," Father Charles continued, "I don't think forgiveness is possible. Unless that occurs, you are continually victimized and pulled into a whirlpool that doesn't seem to go anywhere but down. When you forgive, you are again able to take control, rather than letting the perpetrator of the violence control you."

The Source of Forgiveness

Father Charles Strobel expressed these thoughts on forgiveness: "I do believe that God is ultimately the sole source of whatever good there is in the world. In a simplistic way, forgiveness is good, so somehow it comes from Him. I can say for a fact it came from God through our mama. She taught us as kids that life's too short. When we fought I can still remember her telling us we should forgive and forget."

Like most siblings the Strobel children had their fights. Charles recalls the time she fell to her knees and prayed out loud, "God, help me to raise these children! Sweet Jesus! They're killing each other!"

Mrs. Strobel's litany of "forgive and forget" was etched into her children's subconscious minds. It was the positive influence which carried them through this benumbing ordeal.

A year before Mary Catherine's death, the parents of a sixteen-year-old girl who had been raped and murdered were roundly criticized by family and friends. The mother and father had publicly forgiven their daughter's rapist-murderer and had even been visiting him in prison. One of their acquaintances was quoted as saying, "That's disgusting and ridiculous. They shouldn't have anything to do with the bum. He mutilated their daughter, and now they're paying homage to the monster! That's an unforgivable deed."

Charles had a message for those parents:

I sympathize with them, but I think they believe as I do that forgiveness is a form of love—one of the highest, if not the greatest, kinds of love. . . . The marvel of forgiveness is, if we can continue to love in the face of adversity, love reaches its greatest level. Love can break through the strongest barriers of hatred. Apparently, the family you talked about has a heavy supply of love and is an example of what forgiveness can really do.

As Jerry Strobel soon found out, forgiveness is not the most popular response (even from "religious" people) to a murderer. "I know some people criticized us for forgiving the killer, but that's our position, and we will stand behind it. . . . Some folks say, 'I'd be vengeful,' but you don't know. It's like the old Indian prayer, 'Grant that I may not criticize my neighbor until I have walked a mile in his moccasins.' "

After my interview with Father Charles, he handed me a copy of his mother's funeral mass transcript. "This should be in your book, Jerry." I agree. Here is an excerpt.

As devastating and empty as her death is to us—and it is the hardest thing we have ever done—we must paraphrase her words. God is going to help us. Our Mama will always be there to watch over us, and we need to stay together. Now, two days later as we return to our homes, there will still be great, great needs all around us, and we must try to respond to them as she would want us to. "It can be done," she said. "It must be done," she said.

Forgiveness is possible. The Strobels are living examples of its practicality in a world where it seems easier to say, "I hate you," instead of the words Mary Catherine Strobel instilled in her children: "I really do forgive you!"

Aftermath

William Scott Day, Mrs. Strobel's alleged murderer, was extradited from Texas to Tennessee in July 1988. It had been over a year since I had spoken to Jerry and Charles about the tragedy. The story, which had been dormant, had resurfaced and was front-page copy once again. The *Tennessean* newspaper had obtained Day's confession to the murder—a graphic description of her death. Once again, the Strobels were pursued by the media for the family's reaction. The family refused lest their comments would affect Day's trial.

Naturally, I felt awkward about setting up another interview, but Jerry arranged a meeting at Charles's church. When I met with Jerry and Charles, they were congenial as always.

Initially, the brothers talked about their emotions relating to stories appearing almost daily. Charles said: "Many of the stories that have come out since she died have been surprises to the family. . . . I think to myself, *Oh, no, what am I going to have to do now?*

"We also had to protect the feelings of very good, and in many cases, elderly friends of our mother. For instance, last weekend we had to call their children and warn them about the story before it came out," Jerry earnestly joined in.

Not only did the Strobels have to cope with their own pain, but also with the hurt of friends, even acting as a cushion between their mother's friends and the media. Jerry and Charles are bothered, at times, with the seeming insensitivity of the media. "It happens, for instance, after wrecks or fires. Some reporter will stick a camera in front of the victims and try to get some comment for the six o'clock news. But these victims may not even know what they are saying at the time. In our case, the Sunday newspaper story would have come out in the trial, and that's normally where you'd hear the details. Apparently the paper got hold of it and decided to run the confession."

Charles reflected on the grieving process, explaining that you think of your departed loved one every day. "I think you can revisit her life and her death privately, or with your family or friends. In time you can find more joy in life and move on. You do that at your own pace and with whom you choose."

"But," he interjected, "when families are victimized by murder and the court proceedings drag on, you are subject to scrutiny, and you must go through all of this publicly. This does bother us."

"On the other hand," Father Charles continued, "we have gained a great deal of support. We were blessed to have her as a mother. We didn't know how extraordinary our mother was until the attention was focused on her. We thought she did what all mothers are supposed to do—love their children and help the needy."

After reading the gruesome details of Day's confession, I asked if they could still say "I forgive you" to the killer. Jerry had tried to put the man out of his mind. "I haven't thought about him. He's like a runaway locomotive or a bolt of lightning. What is important is our mother's life—and I've thought about her daily. . . . I just have no feeling one way or another towards him. I know the man has problems. Maybe some people don't know how I can say that. I've just kept it to myself when someone tells me, 'I'd kill him,' or "I'd shoot him and hang him up by his ears!' "

Charles still wonders what prompted the killing. "I still ask myself what there is in someone to bring about this kind of action. Reading this article made me think about our mother, not the killer. Both Jerry and I know how frightened she was. We knew she would have talked to him about us (in his confession, Day reported that Mrs. Strobel said that one of her sons was a priest). We knew she would have cooperated with him. Our mother taught us to cooperate with others and just 'give them whatever they want and go right along and do whatever they say.' Before we read the grisly details, both of us knew what she was going through. We just hadn't seen the incident spelled out in such a graphic portrayal. But, just as our mother would have wanted, I think of her killer in terms of prayer. I think he deserves our prayers."

Charles leaned back in his chair and chuckled, "Mama would have said, 'Charles, he didn't mean it. Poor fella, maybe his father and mother didn't treat him right.' She wouldn't dwell on someone's failures. She could always find something good. I wish you were interviewing her because she had an exciting personality and was a much more interesting character than either of us. She was such a delight to know."

Jerry remarked, "She'd have a peanut-butter sandwich and say it was the best ever, even though it was on a stale piece of bread. 'It's good for you,' she'd say. And, if you complained about the hot weather, Mama would probably ask, 'Isn't it a great day—all this clean, fresh air to breathe?' "

"She was the sort of person that *Reader's Digest* could have done a story about," Charles added. "She could light up a room.

Mama had the ability. It's unfortunate you have to talk to us. She would have been your best interview!"

As I sat with Jerry and Charles in the sanctuary, I felt Mary Catherine would have enjoyed the laughter and positive interaction with her sons. She has left a loving legacy. Not only did she help the homeless, the poor, and the less fortunate, but Mary Catherine Strobel gave us two sons who still believe in forgiveness and aren't ashamed to express it.

10
A Father's Forgiveness:
Ricky Skaggs

"I was feeling rage toward the man and tried to cover it up. Andrew, being the sweet soul he is, let me know I wasn't in a forgiving state of mind."

Ricky Skaggs and son Andrew

Photo by The McGuire Photography Co., Nashville

In the course of an hour, the police scanners in the newsroom came to life: "There's a drowning at Old Hickory Lake. It is believed to be the body of the ten-year-old retarded boy we've been looking for," the voice boomed from the speakers. Minutes later, another dispatcher urgently reported, "A baby has been critically burned. We need immediate transportation." As if that weren't enough, the communications center issued a bulletin: "A multiple pedestrian accident has just occurred. There could be several deaths. All available units respond."

Acting on instinct, our Assistant News Director Buddy Sadler grabbed the two-way radio. "Let's roll on the accident on Murfreesboro Road," he ordered one of the street reporters. When the reporter arrived on the scene, we learned what price anger can extract . . . at the expense of others.

An out-of-towner had tried to cut in front of another car. That pushed the second driver's anger button. He was dead set on getting even. As he tried to catch up with the first vehicle and pass it, the angry driver lost control of his car. It overturned and rolled over four women who were walking along the shoulder of the road. Three of them died!

Death—what a price to pay for one hot-headed person's attempt to lash out at another human being.

While I was writing this chapter, the wire services ran a story that was both bizarre and scary. In Chicago an elderly woman eased her spotless Mercedes into a parking place. As she was carefully maneuvering the shiny vehicle, a young fellow zipped his car behind hers into the same spot. When he jumped out of his car, the woman yelled, "Hey, that's my place!"

"Oh, tough luck, Lady," he snickered back. "Find your own spot!"

At that moment, her anger bomb detonated. The woman hit her accelerator in reverse and rammed into the guy's cherry-red Corvette—not once but again and again.

Who wins in a fit of anger? No one. What's ironic is that most of us know better. Maybe the elderly lady with the Mercedes is a regular churchgoer, and I'd be surprised if her minister had never preached about forgiveness in one of his sermons. Yet, hearing about forgiveness is vastly different from practicing it in our lives. If we did forgive, the results would be staggering. There would be fewer divorces, fewer deaths, and far less stress in our lives. If only we could say "I forgive you" when something takes place that angers us, it would be our stopgap switch. We would be able to catch ourselves before letting the anger build up inside and then erupt.

Too often I become angry and say things I later regret. If you're a parent, you've probably had your anger button pushed a number of times. I still remember that afternoon when my son Jeffrey had scraped the side of my spick-and-span car. I had repeatedly cautioned him to walk his bike by the cars. Instead, he would zip by with a key stuck in the right front handle bar. Jeffrey wasn't steering the bike too well. The key carved a seven-inch gash into my car.

When I walked outside, the gash glared at me. *Oh, no, this can't be,* I muttered to myself. "Jeffrey," I hollered, "how many times have I told you not to race your bike by the cars?" At that specific moment I was hopping mad! I could have sentenced that boy to Siberia for the next ten summers (and winters too!). All the anger inside was racing through me. All kinds of negative emotions were pulsating in my head. I directed my rage at the bike. I picked it up and threw it against the garage. I was paying the price of anger. As I later found out, I paid the price to repair both the car and the bike. It would have been far cheaper (and an example of better parenting) to say, "Son, I forgive you. Next time, take the key out of the handle bar. But for now you're grounded."

So, what's the answer? How can we find the power to forgive at the time we really need it—before we let our emotions run wild? Sure, we can talk about forgiveness but are we sincere or merely paying lip service to the ideal?

The Power of Forgiveness

Ricky Skaggs of country music fame was at his Hendersonville,

Tennessee, home when an emergency call came from a Roanoke, Virginia, hospital.

"I'm sorry to tell you, Mr. Skaggs, but your son Andrew has been shot in the face, and he's in critical condition. A truck driver shot at your ex-wife's car, and the bullet entered the boy's mouth."

Feeling as if the entire universe had fallen onto his shoulders, Ricky could barely talk. "But did they catch the guy?" the young singer desperately wanted to know.

"No, he's still being sought," was the response.

Ricky froze. The shock was so intense, he almost passed out. After several minutes the singer ran outside, dropped to his knees, and screamed to God, "Who would want to hurt my little boy, Lord? I've put my trust in You? Why did You let this happen? Why? You promised me You would always watch over my kids!"

After he calmed down, Ricky felt he had an answer from God. His son, he was assured, would be all right. Ricky immediately chartered a plane and flew to Virginia. More than all else in the world, Ricky wanted to be at his boy's side. Sitting alone in the plane, Ricky kept praying, "Please, Lord, I want Andrew to live! Please make it happen! Please don't let me down!"

The air time seemed like an eternity. When the plane landed, Ricky was rushed to the hospital. As he stepped off the elevator, Andrew's doctor and a policeman approached him. "This is the shell we've taken out of your son, Mr. Skaggs," the doctor told him. "Don't worry, Andrew will be fine. He'll be here with us for several days so we can check on his condition." The policeman hastily added, "And we got the guy who did this to your boy."

"The most important thing was for me to be by Andrew's side," Ricky later told me. "Believe it or not, I wasn't full of hate at the guy who shot him. I hadn't felt revenge. At least, I didn't think I had."

Ricky learned plenty about himself in the next couple of days. During his second day in the hospital—about one o'clock in the wee hours—Ricky and Andrew talked about the shooting.

"Son, someone who hurts people like that is really, really sick.

But they've caught him now," Ricky explained to Andrew. Ricky wasn't prepared for Andrew's amazing response.

"Well, Daddy, we need to pray for him and forgive him because he don't know Jesus," the youngster quietly advised. Ricky testified that Andrew's answer "wiped me out."

"I felt I had been grabbed and shaken for a minute. Like, this is reality and exactly how God wants you to handle it," the singer remembered. "I had to admit, I did have some rage and potential hate building up inside for the guy. Looking down at Andrew and seeing the thirty-eight-caliber bullet hole through his face with stitches everywhere and blood flowing out of his mouth was a horrible sight. And knowing the terrible trauma my ex-wife had gone through . . . What can I say?"

"I was feeling bad things about the man," Ricky admitted. "But when Andrew talked to me of forgiveness, I knew where I stood. I was the one who needed to repent! I was feeling rage toward the man and tried to cover it up. Andrew, being the sweet soul he is, let me know I wasn't in a forgiving frame of mind." Of all the people around, Ricky's seven-year-old son helped his father understand the power of forgiveness.

Ricky went on, "You can say 'I forgive' all day long, but unless you picture yourself and the person you're wanting to forgive, it just won't work. Take that person to the Cross with you in your own mind. I saw myself with my arm around that man and asked Christ to forgive me for the way I felt. You can say 'I forgive' hundreds of times, but your subconscious isn't forgiving. The only way to reach complete forgiveness is through the Lord.

"I know that from another experience. A few months ago, a friend asked me to forgive him for something he had done. I said, 'Sure, everybody makes mistakes, and it's one of those things that can happen in life. Look, I forgive you.' But a week later when his name was mentioned, the hair rose on the back of my neck. I couldn't figure out why I had felt this way toward my friend. I thought I had forgiven him. I finally asked the Lord, 'Why do I feel this way? I've forgiven him.' The Lord spoke to me and said, 'No, you haven't forgiven him. You said you want to forgive him.

But you know you have to come to *Me* for forgiveness. Forgiveness is only through *Me*.' I realized that total forgiveness comes from the Lord. That's where the cleansing comes from."

The more Ricky talked about forgiveness, the more I kept asking myself, *Would I forgive someone who purposely hurt my wife or kids? I mean, it's one thing to hear Ricky Skaggs tell his story, but when it hits close to home, could I do what he did?*

As he was being called onstage at the Grand Ole Opry House, I thanked him for the interview. Before leaving, though, I shared my feelings with him.

Leaning over to pick up his guitar, Ricky looked me straight in the eyes. "You know what's going to happen if you hold the hate inside?" he probed. "If you don't let go of bitterness and hate, *you're* the one who gets eaten alive by the poison. The roots of bitterness hold the tightest of anything. You've got to figure if you're going to grow. There are a lot of Christians who can't figure out why they can't grow and get closer to God. It's that bitterness, but there can be deliverance from that and any barrier in a person's life."

As I drove home after the interview and listened to Ricky singing his hits on the Grand Ole Opry radio show, I reflected on little Andrew's convicting words to his Dad. Ricky's attitude reminded me what a survivor of a Nazi concentration camp wrote: "Bitterness defeats life. Forgiveness carries it on."

When I reached home, I recalled the gash on my car and the broken bicycle. With Ricky's conversation fresh on my mind, I reached out to Jeffrey and hugged him.

"Son, when you do something wrong, I'll always forgive you," I whispered to him.

"I'll forgive you, too, Daddy," he joyfully answered.

Wherever Ricky Skaggs shares his testimony, it makes a difference!

Part III:
The Achievers

11
Acceptance:
George Allen

"My prayer as a recovering alcoholic is very simple: God's will is my life. I want to do God's will."

George Allen

Photo by David Rogers

Motivational seminars are helpful. Yet, I have seen a few of them turn into circuses and pep rallies—five hundred rah rahs, and the session is over.

Yes, we ought to have inspiration, but what kind? Jumping up and down, forcing a smile on your face, and ordering yourself to be happy all the time—as some of these speakers advocate—is ridiculous. This form of motivation has no long-term effect and is not realistic. In addition, it can create unnecessary guilt when life is not always fabulous.

What's the answer?

Forget the fast-acting, expensive medicine show. Look around your community and rediscover what I call "the real people." You can find them easily. Drive to a hospital and ask the receptionist for volunteer services. Meet several of the volunteers, take them out for a break, and discover what motivates them, what makes them tick. It will be an adventure guaranteed to afford you more zip and inspiration than any top-notch motivational speaker. Why? Because you are seeing inspiration/motivation for yourself and not through the eyes of someone who supposedly has a five-point plan on how to make you and everybody else happy for the rest of your lives.

Some of the most inspirational people are in Alcoholics Anonymous. "Wait a minute!" you might be protesting. "I'm not into booze or drugs. Why waste time with a recovering alcoholic?" Simple! Most of them, if not all, have hit rock bottom—sunk lower than you could ever imagine. So low that even you might have considered suicide if you had been in their shoes. But they didn't kill themselves. Instead, they bounced back.

Most alcoholics and drug addicts have visited this wasteland, and it is not an exclusive club. Anyone—rich and poor, young and old—can join the ranks of those who hit the pits. The hope for any of us, including the alcoholic and addict, is the desire to cling to life when it seems to have no meaning and has become as empty as a water hole in the desert.

One of my favorite books as a kid was a compilation of famous quotations. It included the words of the great orator Edward

Everett Hale. This seven-line quotation has opened my heart and mind to the power of living.

> I am only one,
> But I am one.
> I can't do everything,
> But I can do something.
> And what I can do that I ought to do,
> By the grace of God,
> I shall do.

When I arrived in Nashville and reinitiated "I Love Life," the first guest I interviewed reminded me of Hale's quotation. His name is George Allen, and he had been through a living hell. Yet, he wasn't ashamed to talk about it.

"I was a great con as a kid," the distinguished-looking alcohol treatment counselor told me. "My parents were too good to me, and I'm sad to say I took advantage of them," he continued.

As we strolled the grounds of the Cumberland Heights Alcohol and Drug Treatment Center, George nodded to one of his counselees. "You know, he's not much different from me. The only difference is I've been off the bottle for thirteen years, and he's been dry for a month. I've been fortunate over the years. I pretty much messed up my life and still managed to piece it together with the help of prayer."

As we sat on a lawn bench, George breathed deeply and smiled. "I don't want to sound like one of those happy guys you mentioned. But isn't life great? Just to be here and appreciate what we have is awesome to me." Surrounded by a grove of trees, the recovering alcoholic was at ease with himself and life.

But, as he had openly confessed, George had spent years on the street as a "drunk" before arriving at a turning point in his life. When he was in his early fifties, a time when most adults are thinking about retirement and adding up their successes, George was wandering around downtown Nashville. He didn't live in an apartment or hotel. His home was under bridges and viaducts.

George was considered a "wino"—without money, family, and friends.

"How, then, did you dig yourself out of the gutter and into a job that has won you national recognition?" (Several years before our interview, George was named "Counselor of the Year" by the National Association of Drug Abuse Counselors.)

The slow-talking counselor immediately began to track down the roots of his problem. "The recognition isn't as important as what I've been through and how I can relate that to the clients I work with. For me, my triumph from the bottle wasn't overnight. The problem began when I was a youngster and kept getting worse when I became an adult."

Many alcoholics have certain childhood factors in common. George was out of step with the other kids. He didn't know how to make friends or get along. But once he discovered booze, he was hooked. At least he had found a "friend." He thought. "I could be anybody I wanted to be, and do anything I chose to do, I felt at the time.

"I had been uncomfortable with myself since I was nine years old. I didn't like the way I looked. I was short, wore glasses, and tried without success to talk with the girls. But, man, when I drank, what a thrill! I became the greatest-looking and best-talking guy in the world. There was no limit anymore."

But the alcohol wasn't cheap. When he wasn't working (which was often), George tapped into a guaranteed financial source—his parents. But after his mother died, George's financial problems mushroomed. "My father had to go to a nursing home, so I sold their home and gave him some money. I kept the rest. But when the cash was gone in about twenty days, so was I. Little George was lost. There wasn't one relative who would lend me a dime or offer me a place to sleep."

Alcohol had a hefty price tag. His wife and three children left him. The odd jobs were few and far between. While the money supply dropped to almost nothing, his addiction to the bottle was becoming worse. From 1956 to 1972 he couldn't hold down a job. He was on the streets, in the jails, and in work houses. His only source of income was the plasma bank. He'd sell his blood and buy cheap wine. George conned his way into the Union Rescue Mission, but his drinking forced the director to put him out. The fifty-two-year-old drunk was about to hit the skids.

George remembers shuffling down Lower Broad and being picked up by the police as he was coming out of a blackout. He had a fifth of wine in his hand. The officers let him keep it as they whisked him off to the drunk tank. But he soon felt like Chicken Little with the sky falling all around him.

He began to hallucinate and imagine his cellmates were plotting to kill him. "They were arguing about how they were going to do it. I went berserk!"

The jailer ran to the cell and called for a backup. "Get that nut out of here," one of the inmates yelled to the guards. George was shoved outside to a waiting police car but had to stand in the pouring rain as the officers took their time.

On his way to the hospital emergency room, George was tightly squeezing his Social Security card. He was wearing a ragged T-shirt, worn-out khaki pants, and a pair of old tennis shoes with holes. Those were his only possessions in the world.

After a quick checkup, George was given a dismal diagnosis. "Mr. Allen," the doctor advised, "you have a bad case of double pneumonia."

The doctor wrote a note for the jailer. George was sent back to the drunk tank. After the jailer read the doctor's note, he yelled to the guard, "Throw out that Allen guy. He's got pneumonia. Everybody in here is gonna get sick."

There he was, shivering in the cold rain, with no place to go. The rapidly aging alcoholic had bottomed out. *Where do I go?* he wept. *Dad's in a rest home and can't take care of me. I got no family, no friends, no money.*

George was scared and he wasn't craving alcohol. The downtrodden fellow wanted a place to stay. *Maybe if I beg the mission to let me stay there,* he thought, *I can at least sleep there tonight.*

George wandered down to the mission. "Please take me in. I

have no one and no place to go," he pleaded. "I'm sick, and it's cold outside."

"All right, George," one of the workers responded, but no booze this time."

George was practically asleep before his exhausted and sick body touched the bed. The next morning he was escorted to the hospital. He was a physical and mental wreck, shaking like a leaf.

"Please, Lord," he prayed. "Help me make it. Please get me out of this lousy mess!" About that time, a man approached George in the emergency room. George had seen him before at the mission. The man made arrangements for George to enter a center for indigent alcoholics. He walked in a rainstorm to the center.

Once he was there, though, George wanted a drink. *I'll slip away, and nobody will notice,* he said to himself. It kept on raining for three days. He was bored with the center and desperately craved a drink.

As the days slowly passed, a counselor talked with him. She put her hand on his arm. Without thinking, George jerked away from her. He thought of himself as an "untouchable."

"George," she calmly explained, "if you let us, we will help you and even love you."

"This can't be," he retorted. "No one has said a kind word to me in years."

George stared at the counselor. When the two made contact, his years of stuffing everything inside were about to come to an end. He wept. "You really want to be my friend and help me?" he questioned her.

"We do, George, but it's all up to you. You can't allow yourself to live in self-pity anymore."

That was George's crucial moment. He was at the bottom of the barrel, but for the first time he really wanted out. "I hunger to have a good life without whiskey," he said. "Please show me the way."

In Full Gear

George's battle to overcome his addiction was in full swing. He spent thirty days in the center's program. After that, he agreed to stay in a halfway house. But there was a hitch. He had to find a job and pay room and board. George did—for the next year and a half. But working was secondary to his volunteer work at the house. George was assisting the other boarders in upgrading their discharges from the service. For the first time in his life, he was performing a service for others. That caught the attention of a halfway house employee. "George," a counselor asked him, "have you ever thought about being a counselor? You work well with the others here."

"You're kidding," George answered. "I'm an alcoholic and fifty-four years old. I'm too old and not qualified to do anything. I can't possibly do it."

"Easy now," the counselor came back, "you've done more for people than some professional counselors. You've been through hell and have come back to care about others."

After that conversation, George was invited to work in a family program twice a week. Within several months, he was offered a full-time counseling position. After eight and a half years on the staff, he was hired at the Cumberland Heights Drug and Alcohol Treatment Center. He also remarried. George's street days were over!

"I was unable to help myself for years," he calmly tells his clients. "My problem, just like yours, is our inability to know what alcoholism is. I describe the addict as being powerless over the drug. Because of the chronic powerlessness, we are unable to manage our lives. It has become a condition and an illness."

"That's a nice, clean answer, Mr. Allen," one of the clients rebuts him at a therapy session. "But I still drink and don't know how to stop."

George has heard alibis like that hundreds of times before. "Alcoholism is not a passive thing. You must put certain principles into action. That's what these self-help books about alcoholism have in common. They're telling the reader to do something. The reader responds, 'That's great! I believe I'll try that.' Some do for a day or two. And then they start back into everyday life and stop practicing recovery. But recovery from a chronic illness requires daily practice of a set of principles that are not our own. These principles come from a power greater than ourselves, and we, as recovering alcoholics, must practice them. Prayer is among them. I used to pray for God to get me out of the mess I was in. That was all wrong. My prayer as a recovering alcoholic is very simple: God's will is my life. I want to do God's will."

"The key to recovery for me," he skillfully points out, "is my work as a counselor. Helping others is my method of staying clean. It's poetically speaking 'carrying the message of hope to another drunk.' "

Apparently, George's message has been heard across the nation. In 1986, the one-time practicing alcoholic and street person was asked to wait in his supervisor's office for a phone call. As he picked up the telephone, George heard the caller identify himself as a representative of the National Association of Alcohol and Drug Abuse Counselors. "Mr. Allen, I have some good news for you. You have been picked as 'Counselor of the Year.' Congratulations!"

Like most humble persons, George found it difficult to believe he was being honored. He was invited to Atlanta to accept the award at the Association's annual convention.

"I had never worked for recognition since I had been in recovery. I had done what I believed in to the best of my ability. I felt it had been God's will."

George Allen is no longer wasting away under bridges or hiding in vacant cars. He is sixty-seven years old and has a loving wife, a home, and a rewarding career. But the gray-haired counselor has not forgotten where he was thirteen years ago. It is still fresh in his memory. "I'm not in control and will never be in control," he emphasized. "I practice a set of principles in my daily life, and one of them is carrying the message of hope!"

After we had chatted for several hours, George recited a motto:

"When I'm not practicing my recovery program, I'm practicing my disease." "Can you put that in your book?" he asked.

"Sure, George. Who should I attribute it to?"

With a broad smile, he declared, "It's mine. I made it up. It's been a part of my life for years."

No doubt his motto will be carried on for generations by the people he has counseled.

Postscript

Several months after I met George, I heard he had undergone a heart attack which necessitated a triple bypass operation. Out of the blue, George called me to report cheerfully, "Jerry, I just want you to know I've been thinking of you, and I'm doing all right.

I had been thinking of George, too. He had made me feel better about myself and had even inspired me to write a poem. It is my effort to thank him for letting me into his life.

> Take me as I am.
> I'm not perfect, and certainly not all knowing.
> But in God's image,
> Like everyone else,
> I am unique and special.
> Maybe I am indecisive and even frustrated at
> myself and others at times,
> But I accept responsibility for my actions
> in life.
> Some of them might be mistakes I've made,
> But others are goals and dreams I believe in.
> Don't take them away from me.
> You see, in the Spirit of God,
> I accept myself as I am,
> And that makes life so much better!
>
> —J. D.

12
Honesty:
Rae Unzicker

"I didn't talk until I was twenty-five years old. . . . I said, 'Hello,' 'Good-bye,' 'Pass the salt,' and that was about it. The medication got hold of my brain and wouldn't let go."

Rae Unzicker

Photo Courtesy of Rae Unzicker

Don't Be Fooled by Me

Don't be fooled by me.
Don't be fooled by the face I wear,
For I wear a thousand masks that I'm afraid
    to take off, and none of them are me.
Pretending is an art that's second nature with me,
    but don't be fooled, for _____ sake don't be fooled.
I give the impression that I'm secure,
    that all is sunny and unruffled with me
        within as well as without,
    that confidence is my name and coolness my game;
    that the water's calm and I'm in command,
        and that I need no one.
But don't believe me. Please!

—Anonymous

It was one o'clock in the morning, and I couldn't sleep. Ideas and work assignments swam in my head. The Sandman still eluded me. So, I followed the advice of sleep experts—I climbed out of bed.

Somewhere between being awake and asleep, I stumbled to my desk and opened my "I Love Life" file. I thumbed through the names of hundreds of people I had interviewed over the past decade. I counted people instead of sheep.

As I started rereading some of the scripts, I was again captivated by the story featuring a friend, Rae Unzicker. She lived more than nine-hundred miles away, and I had not seen her in a long while. But in the middle of the night, I thought about how much she was willing to help other people if they could become more honest with themselves.

Ironically, I had been one of them. If I felt down and wanted to recoup, she always had time for me. I had often asked her, "Rae, would you mind if we get together for coffee?" I was always sheepish about it. "There's something bothering me, and I just need someone to talk with." She never answered no.

Rae's number-one quality, I feel, is sensitivity. She always listened without prejudging. She opened her ears and her heart.

"Jerry," she would remind me, "don't be so tough on yourself. Enjoy what you have! If you make a mistake, who cares? No one's perfect."

Rae's not afraid to "tell it like it is." She also doesn't sugar coat and play mind games. Maybe that's one reason people are drawn to her. In the past ten years, over five hundred men, women, and children from all walks of life and with every kind of emotional problem have knocked on the Unzickers' door. They've even stayed overnight—and some for a couple of years!

Many were in crisis—an eviction, an emotional breakdown, or a family quarrel. "If you're willing to open up your heart, you might as well open up your house," the former tranquilizer junkie told a reporter from the Saint Paul (Minnesota) *Pioneer Press and Dispatch*. "I've been burned only once when a very good friend in a state of lithium toxicity broke our television set. Big deal." Rae cares infinitely more about people than she does possessions. Others who have looked her up maybe have had a bad day at work or at home and simply wanted to open up their hearts to this compassionate woman who had spent years in mental institutions.

If you're an avid viewer of the major television talk shows, you've probably seen Rae. She has appeared on "Phil Donahue," "Oprah Winfrey," and "Sally Jessie Raphael," among others. As national coordinator of the National Alliance of Mental Patients, founder of a mental-health advocacy project, and a lay therapist, Rae is known to many as "the defender for the rights of mental patients." In her own words, "I think there's a kind of truth and authenticity in the whole area of mental health that you can get only from the experience of having been locked up, drugged, manipulated, lied to, and coerced. It has to do with power, who carries the keys, and who has the rights."

After reading her script, I finally went to sleep. When I reached Rae on the phone later in the morning, I excitedly talked with her about the book. "Rae, you've helped me through some tough times, and I know you can do the same for others once they know you. Would you let me put your story in my book? It can reach someone who might need it."

"No problem," she rapidly replied in her crisp Midwest accent. "If my story can help just one person, let's do it."

A Woman Who Cares

Sixteen suicide attempts, twelve years in four mental institutions, twenty-five psychiatrists . . . After that, Rae was still troubled. Labeled a "crazy lady" by the professionals, she was empty and numb inside. "I didn't talk until I was twenty-five years old," she recalls. "I said 'Hello,' 'Good-bye,' 'Pass the salt,' and that was about it. The medication got hold of my brain and wouldn't let go."

As a teenager in Kansas, she was labeled schizophrenic, psychotic, obsessive-compulsive, and catatonic. That was after she visited her first psychiatrist in the 1950s and was misdiagnosed as mentally ill. Two years later, she made her first suicide attempt and still displays a razor scar on her right wrist from it.

Rae was shipped around to psychiatric wards for the next dozen years. "I was sexually, physically, and emotionally abused in a Kansas state hospital and other places. I have horrid memories of being locked in a room the size of a car with a bare light bulb, a rubber mat, and human waste on the walls and floor." Rae now has a mission to return some power and responsibility to mental patients. She talks graphically about how "my spirit to live was ripped out of me by the daily boredom and tedium." Rae was assigned to "industrial therapy." In other words, she washed dishes six hours a day for six days a week and was given a dollar a month in her canteen account for the labor.

But there was another devastating aspect of the hospitalization she cannot forget. She was kept continually dazed with a smorgasbord of medication and heavy-duty drugs. She has esophagal scars from drinking straight thorazine, which was carelessly given her by a hospital aide.

Released from a mental institution in the late 1960s, Rae found a job but soon fell into deep depression. Without friends and in the pits emotionally, she met a woman who arranged for her to be taken in by a family in South Dakota. That was the beginning of the turnaround in her life, but it didn't happen overnight.

Rae still wanted to kill herself. She swallowed a lethal overdose of pills. Instead of calling for an ambulance and confining her to a mental ward, the family asked five men of faith to come into the house and pray for three days while Rae was in a coma. She recovered, and she joyfully exclaims, "When people ask me whether I believe in miracles, you better believe that I say yes."

After years of being dissected emotionally and mentally, Rae found a therapist who was committed to helping her and who didn't keep her in a constant state of being drugged. He put it plainly, "Rae, I don't like to fail, and your failure will be mine. I care about you, Rae," he constantly reassured her.

Rae still wasn't convinced. In spite of a family and a therapist who cared, she still didn't have the will to live. Again, she tried to kill herself. That was too much for the therapist, who laid it on the line: "Rae, if you ever try to kill yourself again, I'm done with you. You'll just have to find someone else to take you on."

Almost daring him, Rae attempted suicide again. The therapist cut her loose and dismissed her case. "That was the best thing that could have happened to me," Rae tells her counselees. "It was the turning point. I knew it was up to me to accept responsibility for my life—not the mental health system or another human being."

If you've seen Rae on television or visited with her you've probably remarked, "If anybody does, this woman has got her life together." You wouldn't be wrong. The years of her illness have left ugly marks on her, but the beauty of spirit shines through. Her experiences have compelled her to speak out on the mental-health system. The one-time "crazy woman" is touching hundreds of people with her incredible experiences.

When I interviewed her in her Sioux Falls, South Dakota home, a nasty blizzard was gripping the Northern Plains. Sub-zero temperatures (100-below-zero wind chill!) and fierce, unrelenting winds lashed at the windows of her freshly decorated office.

The angry winter storm seemed seasons away as Rae and I sat in the cozy, quiet room. (What a difference from the sterile seclusion rooms she had seen!) Tears, laughter, and confessions from her friends and others in need have come forth within that little office. I know. I've been among them.

Living in Truth and Harmony

You can hardly pick up a book or magazine without running into information on depression. Publishers realize that depression isn't an isolated illness, and that its sufferers are searching for relief.

Dr. Robert Hirschfeld of the National Institute of Mental Health states that depression strikes people who are in their most productive years, "when they're parents of young children, when they're in the midst of developing their careers."

Dr. Martin E. P. Seligman, a professor of psychology at the University of Pennsylvania, has observed that people born in the last thirty years face three to ten times the risk of major depression than their grandparents encountered. The average age for the first attack has dropped in that time frame from the early thirties to the early twenties in age. "There seems to be something about modern life that creates fertile soil for depression," Seligman noted.

Depression is the third most common of all health problems in the U.S.—after cardiovascular and muscular-skeletal diseases. Depression perhaps affects 9.4 million Americans during any six-month period, according to the American Psychiatric Association. Without treatment, symptoms can last for weeks or even years. Treatment seems to help over 80 percent of the sufferers, the APA further reports.

Rae isn't surprised with the figures. "It's really a cliche, but the most common difficulty of this generation is the lack of self-esteem. There are as many reasons as there are people who lack self-esteem. It's easy to say a sad childhood, a bad experience, even a rape, or a death in the family causes the problem. But it's usually not that simple. Lots of us, like I did, look for the answers outside.

"We live in a society that pushes quick fixes. . . . The truth is, there's no quick fix; no magic, easy answer. Most of your answers come from living in truth and harmony with yourself. When you do that, you're free to communicate with other people and accept their own truth, harmony, and love in an openness without expectation. That may sound sappy, but it's true."

Rae is irritated about many products and programs which offer overnight relief from every kind of emotional ailment to instant happiness. "We live in a world that promotes a belief that we have instant access to anything we want. On the other hand, people spend enormous amounts of time and energy avoiding pain and experiencing even the tiniest amount of depression. But they shouldn't forget that there could be some very valuable and meaningful lessons you can learn from feeling bad every now and then. That's just an aspect of being human.

"When I think back, I have memories of good times and the applause I hear when I give a good speech. But the experiences I have grown the most from have been very painful—the many suicide attempts, the desolate periods of loneliness. If we can settle down enough and stop trying to avoid these emotions, learning to accept them as part of the process, we can even start to celebrate pain, sadness, and sorrow. That means we're dealing with ourselves as whole persons."

Is She Cured?

Rae has not been institutionalized for years. She is interviewed on radio, television, and in the newspapers. Her work with mental health has won her national recognition. But the question frequently resurfaces: is she really cured of the unrelenting depression and anxiety that once controlled her?

When I asked her that rather pushy question, Rae leaned forward and shook her head. "When I don't accept that I was ever 'crazy,' it's difficult to accept the idea that I was cured. If you're talking about *cured* in the sense a ham is cured, given time you get better through the process of maturing and ripening. That's really where the root word of therapy comes from—giving it time and the right kind of elements around it.

"I'm frank to say I'm not always together, not the model of

mental wellness. I have emotional problems just like everybody else. But I'm not ashamed of talking about them. That's part of overcoming the denial system that says, 'Everything's great,' when deep inside we know that's not true."

Are there moments when Rae grapples with the past and the memories of the hospitalization, drugs, and loss of control? Yes, there are.

"The worst time in my life," she admitted, "is when I'm hiding in my bed under the covers feeling sorry for myself. Sometimes that can be useful. When I do let that happen, I set a limit and say, 'I'll lie here for twenty-four hours, and then it's up and out, Girl.' When I get up, I don't make any magnificent gestures. Instead, I'll bake a batch of chocolate-chip cookies and share some with a friend; maybe I'll call someone out of town I haven't talked to in a long time, read a book I've been saving, or write a letter to someone and say 'I've been hurting and need *your* help.' I also might put on some music, go for a walk, look at nature, sing—real simple things, because that's what life is."

Then Rae moved into one of her main approaches to wholeness —the fact that a person must choose to enjoy and savor life and answer no, as often as possible, to negative feelings. "But the key word here is choice. My recovery began when I got up in the morning and said yes to life. To exercise that power and use it is the greatest thing we can do for ourselves and the world.

"So there are two sides to the question. Yes, we do have the power to choose and as we do that, we need to be mindful there are people who believe they don't have that power. In that category I would place people incarcerated in mental hospitals, which was my own case. I vividly recall the days I was locked up in seclusion. I told the doctors I wanted to become a writer, and that apparently was not the right thing to do. And there was a girl I'll call Nancy who spent seventeen years in seclusion! She was tied to a chair because she didn't have enough muscle tone to hold herself up. Her power was obviously taken away."

As the wind slapped the window panes harder, Rae's voice became stronger. Her heart overflowed. "If you want to live, really live," she enthusiastically affirmed, "you won't find it in a bank account or stocks and bonds. Real happiness comes from giving. When you give freely, without expecting something in return, what you get back is a hundred times better than what you might have expected. It often doesn't come from a source you think it will or hope it will. If I love you and expect you to love me back the same way, chances are I won't get it. But if I choose to love you, just to love you, then you may love me, or someone else may."

What could I do but sit and drink in this cascade of wisdom and perception born of pain and suffering?

"You also must be willing to take some risks. The way most of us respond to that is to take risks with our finances or jobs, but not taking little risks every day like reaching out to one's spouse or kids and saying 'I love you,' hugging one's kids even if they are thirteen or more (and they usually grimace), and particularly in the case of men, letting qualities of openness and vulnerability show.

"Love," my friend continued, "has been the most helpful and healthy thing I've ever done. Love comes in little notes on the refrigerator to your kids; love comes in sending money to a charity you believe in; love comes in calling a friend you haven't talked to in a while. These things are important in a world where it's easy to get engrossed in an upper-middle-class, upwardly-mobile kind of life-style."

After the interview, I spent about half an hour preparing to reenter the deep freeze with coats, gloves, hats, scarves, and boots. But I already felt warmer on the inside. Rae's story made me feel better about everything—myself, the weather, and life itself.

Many have called her "a lady who cares." That's her way of life. I thank God she's there—offering her love, hope, and honesty to anyone willing to accept them.

Thanks, Rae!

13
Risk:
Don Williams

"This was my dream since I was eight years old. I can't explain why. Most kids like Disney, but my interest was more than that—it was a part of my life."

Don Williams

A friend of mine wanted desperately to succeed in the music business. He has a great voice, plays more instruments than most big-name entertainers, and has a creative knack for writing potentially commercial songs. But he lacks the ingredient to make it: the willingness to take a risk.

Before leaving for Nashville I met him for coffee. He gave me a "demo" tape. "If you meet any producers down there, will you do me a favor and give them this tape?" I assured him I would do my best. But I told him he should be moving to Nashville and selling himself, if that was what he really wanted to do.

"It is," he sadly admitted, "but I'm getting married in a month, and my fiancee would kill me if I told her we had to leave a job with a steady paycheck and move to Tennessee, especially if I didn't have any work lined up there."

Instead, my friend kept his job as a clothing clerk. There was nothing wrong with that, but his job was not personally fulfilling to him. It meant only a paycheck. How unfortunate! At the age of twenty-two years he had already relinquished his dream. He'll always chide himself with: *Just maybe I could've made it. Maybe I could have been writing hit songs and performing around the country.* Unfortunately, the "just maybes" don't fulfill our dreams and aspirations.

But I knew where he was coming from. My family's move to Nashville was a risk. Even though it seemed promising there was still the factor of the unknown—a new city, new environment, new work, new schools for the kids, a new start. But our risk was nothing compared to a middle-aged man who quit a secure job and followed his dream to the fantasy world of Mickey Mouse.

From Banking to Disney

I was among the thousands of news media representatives invited to attend Mickey Mouse's Sixtieth Birthday at Disney World in Florida. The days were packed full of parties, celebrities, and fun. At one of the hospitality suites, my family and I took a break from the heat.

Sitting near us was a man who was sketching what appeared to be Mickey Mouse, and my sons were instantly attracted to him. I introduced myself and inquired about his sketches. "What I'm doing is my life's work. I'm a Disney cartoonist, and I love every minute of it," the happy cartoonist, Don Williams, replied with a warm smile.

Don pointed out the nature of his work—art for television commercials, promotional drawings, and travel around the country drawing for children during special tours. "You're really blessed to be doing what you really want to do," I reacted.

Don broke it down for me. "This was my dream since I was eight years old. I can't explain why. Most kids like Disney, but my interest was more than that—it was a part of my life. As I grew older I just dreamed of going to Disneyland and seeing the films over and over again. Once I got back home I sketched Snow White, Cinderella, and every other Disney character. Unlike other kids, I never outgrew the fantasy world. I wanted someday to get a paycheck from Disney."

The more we talked, the more intrigued I became. Here was a man who didn't sit around and say, "Someday I'll get where I want to be. In the meantime, I'll do what gives me the biggest check and benefits."

For ten years his life had been headed in a different direction. After high school and then four years in the Navy, Don was hired as a bank teller in Springfield, Massachusetts. But his obsession with Disney was stronger than ever.

His first vacation from the bank was spent—you guessed it—at Disneyland. For the next ten years he would rotate vacations between Disney World and Disneyland. "Once I arrived on Disney property, everything came back to me. I just had that fire inside of me to work here. . . . I simply had to be a part of it. I kept dreaming about it, even though I didn't know how to go about it. Here I was . . . a banker who was caught between reality and a dream. For a long time, though, I didn't take any steps to transform the dream into my career."

Soon, Don was named manager of a branch bank, but the promotion didn't give him much deep-down satisfaction. "Sure, it was a very good job, but banking wasn't where my heart was. At the office I'd be nervously waiting to go home where I could sit behind the drawing board and sketch Disney characters. I wasn't your typical pin-striped banker who relished talk about the prime interest rate."

Don was like millions of others who want so badly to do something else. And it becomes an obsession they cannot put aside. Many of them sit around and complain about their misfortunes. They can hardly wait until Friday to leave a job that is unsatisfying and/or nonproductive. Friday is their favorite day of the week, but Monday . . . the worst! Many *dream* of a new career or position, but that's as far as it goes.

Don, now forty years old, was different. He disliked his job but unlike many, he knew exactly what he wanted. For a while he had no idea how to pursue his dream and how far he was willing to adventure. His story is not only that of risk but never-say-die perseverance. He says, "I never had an offer to work at Disney— none at all. No job or guarantee. Nothing except my dream. But that was enough to keep me going until I reached my destination."

The road to Don's success was tough and tedious. For a long time he painted Disney scenes at home on his own time. He thought to himself, *If I don't work at Disney, at least I'll have the pleasure of hanging my portraits in the bank for others to see at Christmastime.* That provided the spark that set the wheels moving.

How Did It Happen?

A local newscaster noticed the pictures at the bank. A collector of Disney art, the newsman was ecstatic over them. Within a few days the fellow visited Don's home (which was wall-to-wall Disney) and taped a segment for his six-o'clock news. After the broadcast, the public response was terrific. Even Don's co-workers at the bank were telling him, "Hey, you're crazy! Why are you wasting your time here when you could be working for Disney?" "Now that the ball had started rolling," recalls Don, "I was going to roll it as far as I could."

One of his friends, a security guard from the bank, was also a friend of the newscaster. The guard sent a copy of the videotape on Don's art to Walt Disney's son-in-law.

The spark was lit, but Don had to fan the flames. In two weeks Don received a letter from a Disney official. They liked the work, but they were not hiring. The letter did, however, direct him to Ralph Kent, the head of the art department at Disney World.

Two months later, armed with a portfolio of sixty of his paintings, Don arrived at his make-or-break meeting with Kent. The Disney executive appeared impressed to the extent that he also wanted to meet with Don again the following day. At that meeting Kent suggested that Don work with Disney artist, Russell Schroeder, by mail. Disappointment showed in Don's face, so Kent made it plain: "Look, I'm not stringing you along. If I wasn't interested in you, I'd tell you right now. If you're willing to work with us on this venture, someday we might have a job for you—but there's no guarantee." That's what Don hung onto.

For a year and a half, that one conversation kept Don in high gear, even though it meant hundreds of hours at his drawing board, without any guarantee of a job. He stuck with it. The first week back in Springfield he did over one hundred drawings and sent them off to Florida.

This was his "mission" in life. When he arrived home from the bank, Don had a quick dinner, and then it was drawing until one or two in the morning. He did that every night, weekends included. After a year he had drawn about every character imaginable—and also began to include paintings.

After those agonizing months, Don made a momentous decision. Although he felt committed to Springfield because he was caring for his mother who was on Social Security, Don quit his job with his mother's blessing. The ex-banker cashed in his pension at the bank, and gave his house to his younger brother with the stipulation that he would care for their mother.

Then, he severed his ties in Springfield so he could move to Orlando to be near the Disney Art Department. He was on his own with nothing but a dream.

"Please Hire Me!"

When Don arrived in Orlando in 1980, there were no open doors and no job offers, not even in the Disney park. He could have found work in a bank. In his words: "I was determined not to get locked into another bank job. I could see myself moving down there, giving up everything, and winding up working in a bank another ten years. I wanted a Disney job, regardless of what it paid."

When he showed up at Disney World, Don went to the casting office. Day after day there wasn't a trace of a job. Don recalls, "I just wanted a job in the Magic Kingdom to hold me over until I could be hired as a cartoonist. I was still planning to submit drawings each week. Only this time, I could hand deliver them instead of mail them." After several months Don was running out of money.

Since there was no work with Disney, he started working as a cashier at a hotel restaurant. Hundreds of Disney employees ate there and received a special discount. It gnawed away at Don. *How come all these people can be Disney employees and I can't be? Do I have two heads or what?* He quit the cashier's job and returned to the Disney casting office. He looked the interviewer square in the face and resolutely announced, "You can't tell me that, after two months, in this whole complex, you don't have one job open doing anything! I mean the Magic Kingdom, the hotels, the wilderness. I don't care what shift or position. You've got to have something!"

Seemingly out of nowhere, two positions materialized, one as a graveyard-shift custodian at a Disney shopping village and the other doing chalk portraits of guests in the park. The latter one was the break Don had been waiting for! Unfortunately, the job lasted only six weeks. The aspiring artist was then reassigned to "Mickey's Mart." Several days later, as Don was stocking shelves in the stockroom, he was called to the Art Department.

Once there Don was told he would be put on a thirty-day trial basis as a cartoonist. If he did well, and they had a position at the end of the period, they would hire him full-time. If no jobs were available, they would know where to find him—back at "Mickey's Mart."

"Naturally, from day one I was a basket case," Don remembers. "The first week I drew Mickey the whole week—Mickey, Mickey, Mickey over and over again. The second week—Donald Duck. The third—Goofy."

Finally the thirtieth day rolled around. The suspense was nerve-wracking. He waited all day long. "Five thirty came around, and nobody said anything. I figured I'd just keep coming back here until someone said something. I went back in on Monday, and no one said anything one way or the other, so I guess I'm permanent." That was nine years ago. Three years later he was promoted to senior artist. And in 1987 the onetime unhappy banker was named Disney senior illustrator.

Dreams can come true . . . Don Williams is living proof.

14
Accomplishment:
Linwood Johnson

"I was ashamed ever since I was in the fourth grade. No, I wasn't a drinker or drug abuser. I couldn't read, and that was my hidden handicap."

Linwood Johnson with then Vice-president and Mrs. George Bush and Sharon Holloway of the Adult Volunteer Literacy Program

Photo Courtesy of Sharon Holloway

"Linwood," his fourth-grade teacher yelled, "you're just plain dumb. You'd better get in gear, or you'll never amount to anything."

Sitting in a classroom over twenty years ago in Rolling Fork, Mississippi, the youngster didn't give much thought to the daily put downs. Why should he? Even though he got Ds and Fs on his report cards year after year, Linwood's instructors sent him on to the next grade. Although his work was below average, the school wasn't paying any attention to Linwood's reading problem.

Why work at all this reading and writing stuff? he thought to himself. *If these people don't care that I can't read or write, why should I? Who needs this learning anyway?*

Two decades later, the energetic Southerner, dressed in formal wear, was standing next to the President-elect of the United States, George Bush, and Mrs. Bush at the Washington Hilton. The middle-aged Mississippian, now from Tennessee, was the honored guest of the Bushes.

So, what on earth could have earned him an invitation to a Presidential event? After all, he was the below-average kid who couldn't read and had given up on himself.

"I was in denial most of my life," Linwood confessed. "I wasn't any different from the drug addict or alcoholic who can't admit he has a problem. I was ashamed ever since I was in the fourth grade. No, I wasn't a drinker or drug abuser. I couldn't read, and that was my hidden handicap."

Linwood was like the other 27 million adults in this country labeled as functional illiterates. They can't read, write, or cope with simple tasks like completing a job application or passing a written drivers's test without cheating. Many of them work at low-paying jobs, living from paycheck to paycheck and bluffing the people around them into thinking they can read. Linwood fit that pattern to a "T"!

"I'm Tired of Being a Loser!"

When he was thirty-five years old, Linwood told himself, *I'm sick and tired of taking a back seat to everyone else. I'm throwing away my life 'cause I can't admit that I have a problem. If only I would learn how to read, the sky could be the limit.* Although he was a custodian at Vanderbilt Hospital and had worked minimum-wage jobs since he quit school, the Nashvillian was determined to take charge of his life.

Linwood swallowed his pride. He walked into his supervisor's office and quietly admitted, "I don't want you to think less of me, but I can't read or write. I can't keep it a secret anymore." Instead of being laughed at or low-rated, Linwood was encouraged by his boss to seek help.

That was Linwood's first step. The next thing he did was call the Metro Volunteer Literacy Program in Nashville. Within a couple of days, he was learning how to read.

"Please Help Me!"

January 12, 1987—6 PM . . . a momentous time for Linwood! His first reading lesson was with Dee Marquardt, his tutor.

"The cat jumped . . . (Linwood meticulously enunciated from the reader's textbook) . . . The cat jumped over . . ."

"That's great, Linwood," Dee reacted. "I know we've got a long road ahead of us, but I know we're going to make it."

Linwood couldn't believe the positive feedback. He was encourged to keep on reading for the first time in his life! That was his inspiration to continue his lessons. In his words, "I was used to being cut down by teachers in school. But it's different now. I'm being praised for every bit of progress I make. I felt like shouting to the world, 'Linwood Johnson won't give up this time. No matter how much it takes, I will read.' "

Linwood practiced, practiced, and practiced. Within a few months, he had completed several workbooks and mastered the alphabet, long and short vowels. His reading level jumped from second grade to fourth. He soon became the program's "star" pupil. In less than a year, his reading level progressed to the fifth-grade plateau.

But that was just the beginning. Linwood regularly met three or four times a week with his tutor at the school. During one of the sessions, a visitor dropped in from the nation's capital.

"Linwood," Sharon Holloway, the Literacy Program director, told him, "this is Barbara Bush. Her husband is campaigning for President. Mrs. Bush is checking out our program."

Within minutes, Linwood was enthusiastically telling Mrs. Bush about his reading successes.

"Mrs. Bush, I've been reading a story about Helen Keller. She couldn't see or hear. She had these handicaps, but she learned to read by writing words in her head! Ma'am, I can see, talk, and hear. If she could read, so can I! Her life encouraged me to keep on going. But if I give up, there's no one to blame but me! No way do I want to wake up five or ten years from now and ask, *Linwood, why did you give up on the reading program?* I'll be giving up on myself again if I do."

As she left the school, the future First Lady told Sharon, "I want that man to do one of the national television announcements on literacy."

Linwood did. His story grabbed hold of the ABC television crew who taped it. One of them later said to Linwood, "You even touched the people in the network editing room." But Linwood's success story went beyond the network announcement. Soon, he was in demand as a speaker. The kid who was kicked around in school by some of his teachers and labeled "stupid" was in the limelight. His message of accomplishment mesmerized audiences. Speaking with pride, Linwood wasn't ashamed of admitting the problem he had been saddled with since childhood.

"It takes a lot of guts for a man or woman of my age to admit to a reading problem. But before anyone can really succeed in this world, he has to have basic reading skills. Sure, I had a tough time facing up to my problem. I was like an addict on the street. Ask him if he snorts cocaine, and he'll say, 'You're crazy. I'm not into that junk.' If you had asked me if I could read a couple of years ago, I would have said, 'Sure can. I'm not one of those illiterates.' But I don't have to lie anymore because *I can read!* I had to quit conning myself and the people around me into thinking I was a reader. I started from scratch as a middle-aged man and learned reading skills a lot of kids have already learned.

"Sure, it's tough to sit in a room when you're thirty-five years old and practice simple words and vowels—but the bottom line is this: I'm living life so much better than ever before. When I get home in the afternoon, I grab something to eat and have a book in my hand until nine or ten o'clock that night. I'm obsessed with reading and love every minute of it."

Shortly before George Bush was inaugurated, Linwood was invited to a National Adult Literacy gala in Washington, D.C. Sharon Holloway made the trip with him. As throngs of guests looked on, the one-time "illiterate" adult was introduced to the President-elect and the future First Lady.

When Linwood walked toward the Bushes, Mrs. Bush quickly responded, "I know you from the television announcement." At that moment, Linwood thought of his late mother and said to himself, *Mama, I wish you could look at your son now!*

The Road Ahead

The glitter and excitement of the event have passed. But Linwood's passion for learning is brightly burning. Several months after the release of this book, Linwood Johnson will be receiving his high-school diploma. I guess some people might not think that's a big deal.

But for Linwood, it's just as important as a business executive signing a multi-million-dollar corporate deal.

When I finished writing this story, I called Linwood at home early one Saturday morning. I didn't know if he'd be awake. But I was excited to hear his reaction to the chapter and to make sure there were no inaccuracies.

"Linwood, did I get you up?" I sheepishly asked.

"No," he perkily responded, "I've been awake since five this morning. After cleaning my place, I started reading the New Testament. You know something, Jerry, I'm a churchgoer. For most of my life, I heard about the Bible from a minister. But now I can read the Good Book for myself.

Before I had a chance to talk about this chapter, Linwood happily declared, "You know, every day is like a weekend or holiday to me. The more I read, the more I learn. My life is just beginning."

After we visited on the phone, I was convinced Linwood's story will go beyond this chapter. My guess is that Linwood Johnson will write a book about his victory over illiteracy. I hope he does. It will prove that a kid who grew up with a "hidden handicap" can accomplish his goals, if he admits his problem and has the grit to face it.

Part IV:
The Survivors

Faith

Dear God,
I was timid and shy.
And yet, I felt a need to communicate.
But inside I really cried.
Call it fear, or even a bad self-image.
It all boiled down to this—stagnation, depression, even
  frustration.

And then one December night we met.
I was reading a chapter of Luke
And these words shot from my mind right down into my spine:
With God nothing is impossible.
With God, nothing is impossible.
With God . . . .
And then, I felt different, almost reborn.
I spent the night thinking, praying, and dreaming
And then the morning came.

I opened my eyes . . . the sunlight from the window frame gained
  momentum
The world seemed to be smiling.
All those negative thoughts and worry didn't matter anymore
'Cause I felt fulfilled with a warm genuine feeling.
With God, nothing is impossible.
I can achieve what I really desire.
From then on, my dreams started to become reality.
Call it what you want
But I call it . . . faith.

                                                    —J.D.

15
Independence:
Rift Fournier

"You might not sit in a wheelchair like mine, but each of us has a 'wheelchair,' an obstacle or barrier of some kind. That's where we have a choice—either deal with it or let it control us."

Rift Fournier with Paul McCartney

Photo Courtesy Rift Fournier

You may remember Willie Nelson's "Farm Aid II Concert." Perhaps because of my Midwest background and my current "Music City U.S.A." connection, a national producer for NBC radio asked if I would cover the event for the network.

"No problem," I replied. "If there is, I'll work it out." I admired Willie for his efforts. Since I am a native of South Dakota, where hundreds of farmers were declaring bankruptcy, I appreciated the fact that Willie was touching the lives of many families I had met and interviewed for over a decade. The country superstar was providing more than money for them. He was making the nation aware of those farmers' daily struggle for survival.

Our family had planned a vacation in South Dakota during the week of "Farm Aid II." We made the lengthy drive to our previous home in Sioux Falls. I cut my visit short after two days, left Linda, Jeffrey, and Jeremy behind to enjoy the rest of the vacation, and flew down to Austin, Texas, for Willie's concert. An adventure was ahead of me.

When I arrived in Austin, I spent most of the day filing material for the network and waited patiently until one o'clock the next morning for Willie and some of his celebrity friends to entertain at a local club. NBC had requested an interview with Willie, and I was assigned to do it. Unfortunately, Willie and his compadres were in no hurry to show up at the club, and I was already running on empty. Making it back to the motel at 2 AM, I called the network and fed a couple of generic stories. After the feeds, I set the alarm for 4 AM and was fast asleep within seconds.

It seemed only a couple of minutes before the alarm jangled unmercifully in my ears. I felt worse than when I had closed my eyes around two hours earlier. I swiftly threw note pads, recorders, mikes, and even a telephone into my suitcase. Soon, a taxi whisked me away to a hotel where the press bus would transport a bunch of groggy reporters to Manor City, Texas, site of Farm Aid II.

As the bus was pulling into the grounds of the Fourth of July extravaganza, the music was already blaring from the stage. Within minutes, Willie strolled onto the stage and announced to the sleepy eyed-crowd, "Welcome to Farm Aid II!" Shortly after that, the familiar sounds of Willie singing his hits snapped the fans to attention. The excitement created a frenzy that maintained its momentum until the last set was over.

But the reporters' assignment wasn't to sit around and enjoy the music with the spectators. We were escorted through a maze of fences and security guards to the rear of the stage. This was the press tent where I would remain until midnight. Dozens of telephones were hooked up, and within minutes the coverage of the concert was being heard and seen around the world.

As the hours plodded along, the sun relentlessly beat down on the crowd. Water hoses were rolled out to cool down the audience. The medics were being called to assist victims of heat exhaustion. The unbearable humidity and temperatures in excess of 100 degrees affected us. No one escaped the blistering sun, not even the news media.

I was immersed in sweat, and my head felt like it was splitting open. The lack of sleep and the Texas heat left me light-headed. I needed a break from the concert and the stories I was being asked to send every hour. I felt as though I would dehydrate if I didn't have a cold drink soon.

When I walked around the tent, I noticed a rugged-looking fellow in a wheelchair. "Hey," he asked one of his crew members in a gruff voice, "any word when we can interview Willie?"

I couldn't help but notice a cooler loaded with soft drinks and ice by his side. He noticed me, too.

"If you want anything to drink," he hollered, "take it." That was an invitation I couldn't turn down! I quickly poured myself a cold drink.

"Are you really here to interview Willie?" I inquired after chug-a-lugging the soda.

"You got it, friend. That's what I do for a living." He then introduced himself as Rift Fournier (pronounced "Fourn'yea"). I had not heard of him but found out that his work as a producer-writer-director was impressive.

He wasn't bragging—simply stating facts. "I've co-produced

the 'Mike Douglas Show' and written scripts for 'Highway to Heaven,' 'Charley's Angels,' 'Kojak,' and 'Wise Guy.' That's only a few of the things I've done," he mentioned when I asked him about his background. "I've even won an Emmy and a Peabody for the NBC children's series, '60!' Here, take a look at my bio, if you want to."

As I read his background sheet, I felt compelled to include his story in "I Love Life." At twenty-four, he was the youngest delegate to the 1960 Democratic National Convention. When he first visited Paris in 1971, he was accompanied by his friend Orson Welles. His most current project was "Cover Story," a magazine-style profile of entertainers (USA Cable Network and in worldwide syndication). He produces, directs, writes, and narrates the show.

What an impressive list of credentials! He has done practically everything he has wanted to do in the past thirty-four years—except one thing so many of us take for granted. He cannot climb out of his wheelchair and walk. One of the articles in his press kit explained his disability:

> Stricken by polio during his junior year in high school, Rift Fournier collapsed when he climbed out of bed one Sunday morning to answer the telephone. He never walked again. But his disability didn't take charge of his life.

As I was looking over his materials, he wasn't shy about telling me of his struggles. "I made a decision back then. No one would treat me like a minority. I finished high school and college. For a couple of years I hit the road as a drifter. I took work when and where I could find it. You know," he chuckled, "I've written jokes for comedians, worked in advertising, and had a whim to wander off to Cape Kennedy (Canaveral). I just couldn't sit around and complain. I still can't."

Rift represents a rare breed of people with "high hopes." That was why he was among the few to obtain an exclusive interview with Willie Nelson. He is a can-do person.

Rift was in an expansive mood. "You've heard the joke, 'I never knew I was poor . . . ' To tell you the truth, I never knew I was handicapped. Sure, I can't walk, but I can scuba dive down eighty-five feet into the ocean or get in a plane and fly to Europe to direct a film. I never thought I was crippled and unable to follow through on my dreams, even if I couldn't reach them every time. So what? At least I tried, and that's the key right there."

As we talked, I wasn't paying any attention to the wheelchair. I was captivated by his presence and the sincerity in his eyes. He wasn't complaining, criticizing anyone, or bragging about himself. He was free of those destructive emotions. He had earned his independence the hard way.

"Hey, Papa," his son Noel reminded him. "Tell him about your Presidential award." I learned that Rift had been honored by President Jimmy Carter as one of the Handicapped Artists of America on behalf of the National Endowment for the Arts.

"I consider myself an artist who happens to be in a wheelchair," he mused out loud. "I'm also a doer who has dreams. Being physically disabled has nothing to do with my talent and determination. I have always been able to get things done. If I try and try, and it doesn't take off, I'll go on to the next project on my priority list. Here's a little test I give myself when I'm analyzing my next step. I determine, first of all, if I really believe in the goal. If I don't, I write it off. Second, there has to be a place or market for the final product or result. I don't follow dreams just to be a romanticist or because my ego says, 'Boy, I have to do that because I'll receive publicity or attention.' I do something with the knowledge that I can sell the product because there's a need for it."

You Can Achieve!

As I was writing this chapter, a horror film was released that sent several disabled groups into an uproar. The grotesque movie depicted a quadriplegic who used a monkey, trained to help severely disabled people, to commit murders. One member of a disabled group that picketed the movie said, "The central insult is that it's another picture showing disabled people as bitter, angry cripples and murderers." One of the signs carried by a protester read, "What next: Attack of the Killer Seeing-eye Dogs?"

Although some disabled people might downplay that movie as just another far-out Tinseltown fantasy, Rift expressed outrage about society's stigma on those with disabilities. "Parents are actually made to feel guilty if they have a disabled child. This is terrible! Many people stand condemned of committing a gross sin against disabled kids. I've seen it hundreds of times. We steal their dreams and don't allow them to believe they could become the President of the United States, a network evening anchor, or any other number of responsible positions. Our system reinforces this antiquated thinking.

"That system," Rift lashed out, "doesn't exclude our school systems—places where the instructors should teach our children about their potential, regardless of what's physically wrong with them."

No amount of writing or speaking will change the attitudes of those who make condescending or prejudicial judgments against a disabled person. This is precisely why we must do all we can to instill a can-do philosophy into our children.

Rift didn't grow up with a crippled mentality and a self-image of being abnormal or less of a person because he couldn't walk. And when he was stricken with polio, he didn't buy into the "poor-me" routine and didn't put himself down.

"More than anything else," Rift emphasized, "I would love to take my attitude and place it in the minds of disabled kids, and especially their parents." It was plain that he earnestly believed every word he was speaking. Several other reporters were eavesdropping on our interview, so his message was going out.

"The kids should understand the world at large doesn't care about their problems. I know that sounds rather crude, but it's true. It's the parents' responsibility to put that across and to encourage independence—and doing as much as they can for themselves."

Rift gazed at the dozens of photographers, journalists, and security people. Shaking his head, Rift motioned toward the crowd. "Many of them won't admit it openly, but each one of them has some type of 'handicap,' something they can't or won't do. That's our common denominator. You might not sit in a wheelchair like mine, but each of us has a 'wheelchair,' an obstacle or barrier of some kind. That's where we have a choice—either deal with it or let it control us."

As Rift grinned at his son Noel, I read pride in the looks they exchanged. "What's great about all my struggles?" he questioned me and then answered for himself. "I wouldn't allow this disability to take away the joy of being a father. Even when Noel was very small, I vowed it wouldn't get in the way of our relationship. But I also had to take some chances with him.

"I still think about the first playground where I took him. There was a jungle gym there. Of course, he was no different from the other kids and was determined to climb to the top. But if he fell, I knew the odds were against my catching him. I also figured it was more important for him to do that than it was for me to stifle him with my fears. Noel needed that freedom just as much as I needed it."

Rift has been climbing "mental" jungle gyms for years. As Rift admits, he has had a strong arm to hold him when the odds have appeared to be overpowering. "I've gone through dark periods when my faith wavered, and it was very painful for me. But I came back to it. I know I'm not in charge of my life. I just have to do what's in front of me. I live today and stay in the here and now. If I worry about tomorrow, it's because of my lack of faith."

After we had talked, Rift's production crew was preparing for the Willie Nelson interview. "Got to go," he said as we shook hands. "I hope your 'I Love Life' idea takes off some day. Maybe you can write a book and make me a part of it."

I thanked him for the interview, the cold drinks, and most of all for the wisdom he had shared with me. He had reminded me, "Don't be afraid of the jungle gym."

Farm Aid II was a superstar's offer to make other lives better—but, even more than the concert, I think about the powerful man in a wheelchair. I understand what he meant by the "mental" jungle gyms. Whatever our dreams are—producing a television show, writing a book, being a loving parent, or simply spreading joy to those around us—we have to take that first step . . . and make the leap of faith.

If you've tried and failed, don't worry. Rift has fallen off as many times as he's reached the top. "If you keep on going, even when everything and everybody are against you," he asserted, "you'll succeed—and by that I mean succeed in feeling good about yourself. That's freedom!"

If that weren't true, you wouldn't be reading about him right now!

16
Achievement:
Jan Wilson

"I just wanted to live without the threat of dying from the tumor. . . . If the amputation meant I could be rid of the cancer and the pain, I knew what had to be done."

Swimmer Jan Wilson being honored by President Reagan at the 1984 International Games for the Disabled in New York

Photo by Bill Teague

"You've got to be insane to interview a bunch of kids with cancer," the brusque producer blurted out. "There's no way I'd go to some camp for them. I couldn't stand to be around that kind of sickness—it depresses me."

What an unfeeling remark! When I started "I Love Love" I had asked a television producer about a news segment featuring terminally ill children at a special retreat. I thought it would be an innovative weekend segment.

"If you do this," I tried to convince him, "the so-called 'normal' kids can learn so much about cancer and leukemia. Most of all, the show can reach the parents of the able-bodied kids and provide a positive forum about disabilities."

My efforts were fruitless. The gruff television veteran was not about to change his mind. "People," he exclaimed, "don't want to see sick kids on the tube. They make the viewer uncomfortable. And, to tell you the truth, I don't think your 'I Love Life' show should even be aired on the radio, let alone on my television station. Besides that, it won't sell. The hard news is where the ratings are!"

I closed my ears to what that television "expert" thought. Unfortunately, as I've learned over the years, his jaundiced position has its backers. Time and time again, my "I Love Life" guests have told me, "You find out who your friends really are when you become handicapped."

According to an attractive, but paralyzed, twenty-one-year-old woman, "Some people don't want to be around me because I can't walk. They won't communicate with me. Instead of asking questions about my paralysis, they give me a song-and-dance routine about how nice the weather is." Unfortunately, adults with preconceived notions about disabilities affect the attitudes of their children. Dr. Alexander Tolor, a professor of psychology at Fairfield University in Connecticut, who has conducted an extensive study of physical and emotional disabilities, states: "The way children respond to someone with a disability is largely dependent upon how the adults around them respond."

When I mentioned my encounter with the producer to a group

of wealthy patrons at an exclusive social club, one of them argued with me. "I have a difficult time thinking that anyone would be that biased against another human being just because he or she has a handicap. That, to me, is really fabricated."

"Ma'am," I cautiously rebutted, "how many disabled people have you known as close friends?"

"Well," she hedged, "I honestly can't say, but . . . "

She had answered her own question. Many people either don't know or aren't willing to become acquainted with a disabled person. Carrying it a step farther, some even turn away from their closest friends if, through no fault of their own, they become disabled. That is tragic. Thousands of disabled people can offer worlds of strength and hope to us, if only we are willing to spend time with them—and they can provide more motivation than any top-drawer speaker could ever offer. One of them, who lives in Greensboro, North Carolina, is an attractive amputee swimmer who inspires by doing.

Harsh Reality

November, 1975—Lexington, North Carolina . . . College sophomore Jan Wilson was anxiously awaiting Thanksgiving dinner at her parents' home. But the smell of turkey was secondary to the ordeal she was about to undergo.

"Jan," her doctor quietly advised her, "you have a tumor growing out of control. We have no choice but to remove your right leg above the knee."

Of course, the diagnosis scared and sickened the bright, athletic college student. She had been a youth league swimmer since the age of eight, and her ambitions of becoming a competitive swimmer would be destroyed. *How can I ever achieve what I've dreamed about with only one leg?*" she kept asking herself.

But Jan didn't dwell on the negatives for long. She realized there was another aspect of the surgery even more important than being an Olympic swimmer. She might have only one leg, but she would be alive! "I just wanted to live without the threat of dying from the tumor," she remembered ten years later. "If the amputation meant I would be rid of the cancer and the pain, I knew what had to be done."

After the surgery and a week's stay in the hospital, Jan was back home. The Wilson home was laden with laughter, love, and support for the energetic twenty-year-old athlete. Yet, Jan was hurting on the inside. *How am I going to be accepted at school? Will my friends still like me? Can I swim again?* The questions multiplied. There were few answers. What she wanted most of all was to tell her closest friends about her fears, doubts, and insecurities. *After all,* she said to herself, *That's what friends are for.*

One of them had called and wanted to drop by her home. Jan thought, *This is my chance to let him know about my frustrations and to be totally open. I want him to know.* But her friend didn't want to listen. He was uncomfortable even being in the same room with her.

"How are you, Jan? Sure miss you a lot," he shakily greeted her from a distance.

"You don't know what I've been going through," she sadly replied.

"I bet," he hastily answered. "Hey, when are you coming back to school?"

"You don't know how it's been since the operation," Jan confided, still trying to pry open the conversation. But her friend didn't want to unlock his self-made door.

"Well, I'm glad you're doing fine. I better leave. See you later, Jan."

Why can't he sit and listen to me? Jan muttered to herself. *We've been great friends before. Losing my leg has cost me his friendship!*

While she was wondering if her one-time best friend would ever return, a casual acquaintance of Jan's re-entered her life. Only this time, the friend was offering what Jan desperately sought. "I think she needed to be needed," Jan says with a smile. "I definitely needed her."

Sherry Garner and Jan had worked together as lifeguards during their high school years, but they hadn't been very close. Surprisingly, the amputation was the key to bringing them together.

"I knew it was hard on Sherry to be with me after the operation. When we carried on a conversation, I saw the sadness in her face. Her eyes would become puffy with tears."

Unlike Jan's former "best friend," Sherry wasn't distancing herself from Jan. Rather, she was drawn to her. Every night Sherry called Jan. On the weekends they would drive to the beach. They were enjoying life one day at a time. Jan and Sherry made a deal—not to be afraid to tell each other anything, even at the risk of offending. That's bona fide friendship. It wasn't phony or superficial. They shared their deepest dreams and innermost thoughts with each other. And they laughed and cried together.

Jan never was defensive about her leg. While strolling on crutches at the beach, she noticed the stares of the crowd. "I had wished at least, if they had had a question about my appearance, one of them would have asked me," she confided to Sherry. On a hot summer day, a suntanned young man did exactly that.

"What happened to your leg?" he carefully inquired.

Neither embarrassed nor defensive, Jan tried to put him at ease with a ready answer. "To tell the truth, a shark got me!" He started to laugh, and so did Jan. The ice was broken. They began to talk about the loss of her leg and why it was taken off.

Jan was learning to approach life step by step. Still, she had another hurdle to cross. Several months after the amputation, she was ready to be fitted for her prosthesis. Her anticipation and excitement were mounting. She had no idea what to expect. "When I was fitted for the artificial leg," Jan recalls, "I was convinced I'd be back to normal and would be able to walk and go back to school." Within minutes of the fitting, Jan was in a state of shock. "There wasn't any magic when I left the doctor's office. I kind of hobbled out. I had to re-learn how to walk."

Jan desperately needed a boost. She wanted to recapture her dream of being a competitive swimmer, but how could she? The young amputee was having enough difficulty merely adjusting to the prosthesis. Why waste time on a vision that couldn't possibly be transformed into a solid goal?

"I Believe in You, Jan!"

As she doubted her potential, a young man entered her life. Bill Teague, an experienced coach and student of human physical movement, met Jan when she re-enrolled in college. When he found out about her background in swimming, Bill was determined to help her return to the pool. "I'll go with you as much as it takes," Bill promised Jan. "I know you can be a great swimmer. But you'll have to practice harder than ever before."

Jan decided she had nothing to lose. The two met at the pool night after night where she persistently practiced. Slowly she regained her confidence, but was it enough to take the plunge in a swimming tournament? "I never thought about competing again," she confesses, "but Bill was giving me the support I needed to take a chance with other amputee swimmers."

Jan was a nervous wreck when she swam in her first tournament. Yet, the jitters rapidly disappeared when she heard the news: "Jan Wilson of Greensboro, North Carolina, has placed first in all the swimming events."

Jan was on her way to the national amputee games. She placed first in every event! From then on, Jan no longer had problems with her confidence. Next, she was chosen to participate in the 1980 Olympics for the Disabled. Jan swam away with the bronze in the 100-meter breaststroke.

Three years later she captured four gold medals and a silver at the Canadian Disabled Games. She was named the Outstanding Female Athlete in the 1983 Nationals. And in 1984 Jan's years of hard work caught the attention of President Reagan. The nation's chief executive handed the North Carolina native the Olympic torch to light the flame for the 1984 International Games for the Disabled.

After the ceremony, she was determined to put every ounce of energy into the events. *Win or lose,* she told herself, *no one can stop me from doing the best I've ever done.* When the games concluded, Jan carried away one gold, three silver, and three bronze medals. She was one of the games' highest total medal winners.

Jan has not stopped winning awards and recognition. Still, the plaques and publicity are secondary to the dream that was reborn in her college years. She hasn't spent much time dwelling on that part of her life. She doesn't have time to waste. She is in the weight room at a fitness center every morning at 5:30 AM. After several hours of working out with the Nautilus equipment, Jan dashes off to work. The work day doesn't end at 5 PM, because Jan is back in the pool at night.

"People in disabled sports have a genuine love of life, and they're focusing on what they can do," Jan was quoted in an article about her in the *Greensboro News and Record.* "It has been a positive approach that has carried over into other aspects of my life, probably forever. Now, when I hear people say, 'I can't do that,' I think to myself, *Have they really tried?*"

But, as she admits, there is another link to achievement. "You also have to have someone behind you. My husband, Bill Teague, is that person." Bill was the college coach who persuaded Jan years earlier to grab hold of her dream and make it come alive.

Jan Is a "Hard News" Story

When hundreds of amputee athletes gathered in Nashville for the Eight Annual U.S. Amputee Athletic Association National Championships, Charles Cook of the U.S. Amputee Athletic Association called me about Jan: "We have really great athletes in town with fantastic stories to tell. There's a young woman from Greensboro, North Carolina, who would make a terrific interview. She's warm and articulate and has a message worth hearing."

As Charles was pitching me the interview, my mind returned to the gruff television producer I had known a decade ago. I wonder how he would have reacted to the telephone call. "Forget it," he would probably have complained. "No one could care less about amputee swimming."

Fortunately, I never bought his sour message. Ten years later, "I Love Life" is still on the air, and so are hundreds of other media programs around the country that feature positive stories.

"Charles," I happily replied, "If you bring her to the station tomorrow morning, I'll put her on a five-part weekly series called 'I Love Life.' "

"Great!" he exclaimed. "Her name is Jan Wilson, and you won't regret making the commitment."

Charles, I *never* had any regrets!

17
Determination:
Fred McBee

"When somebody says, 'I can't do it,' those words push me to show what they really are. 'I can't' is an illusion. There's always a way."

Mr. and Mrs. Fred McBee

Photo Courtesy Fred McBee

I never stopped believing in "I Love Life," even though the "downers" would naively urge, "You need to cut this sweet streak out of your mind and become a real hard-news person." But they had overlooked the genuine success stories of hope and challenge. For instance, a few years ago one of the highest-rated television movies was "The Ann Jillian Story," about the actress-singer who underwent a double mastectomy and fought back with courage and determination. "Highway to Heaven" relates emotional stories with happy endings. The show lacks violence, fast cars, and even a hint of dirt, yet it has consistently maintained high ratings on a commercial network.

Skeptics of the "I Love Life" concept made me more intense about the project. It consumed my thoughts—weekends, weekdays, and holidays. It was part of me and had to be expressed.

Ken Hakuta, one of the world's greatest marketing geniuses, knows what I'm talking about. He wrote in *Success* magazine: "You can inspire people to yearn for your product if you believe you were put on this planet to sell it . . . it is your mission." Hakuta's message is powerful: Believe in the project and in yourself!

I did! But I had also asked myself, *Why would anyone want to read a book of "I Love Life" stories anyway?* But the nagging question never prevented me from following this dream.

Night after night and weekend after weekend I pounded away at my typewriter. I had to release the book from my system. I was no different from a songwriter with stories to tell. "You don't write to make money or to be a success," advised Walter Anderson, editor of *Parade* magazine and author of *Courage Is a Three-letter Word.*

"Write," he counseled, "because you sincerely have something to say from the heart. A book is like a long letter to a close friend. Open up your thoughts and let them flow. Forget about the critics and the Doubting Thomases. Just do it!" Without any guarantees, I knew it had to be done, and I wouldn't stop until it happened.

So, if you want something, however far-fetched it seems, let the dream live. But beware: you also have to believe you were put on this earth for that reason, and people will start believing you.

A Human Dynamo

Fred McBee is a prime example of determination in the face of adversity. He is a human dynamo who loves it when the "downers" sneer, "You're nuts. What you want to do can never be done!" In a class by himself, Fred epitomizes the can-do attitude. He has been a doer since childhood.

Raised in Texas, Fred was immersed in the state's cowboy culture. He competed in junior rodeos and worked on ranches. The lean, aggressive youngster had a vision of becoming a professional rodeo cowboy. He was *determined* to make it happen. At the age of sixteen he wanted to drop out of high school. His parents told him, "If you want to be in the rodeo, you can spend the summer traveling to different ones in the Southwest." But that thrill was short-circuited!

In 1964 Fred was thrown off a horse during a practice session in Oklahoma. Three vertebrae in his neck were broken. He was paralyzed from the chest down. "I went through a wide range of emotions," Fred told me. "At first, you just don't believe it, and then you get pretty angry when you realize it was you. Then, you just get on with it. It's not the greatest thing that's happened to me. But there comes a time when you decide either to overcome or go under. It's pretty clear what your choices are."

Fred spent six months in critical care after the accident. Then he was transferred to a rehabilitation hospital in Oklahoma City where he stayed two years. "Physically and emotionally, rehab was the most intense experience of my life. It taught me about effort, attitude, and perseverance. I studied on my own to pass the G.E.D. for a high school diploma, but the most important goal was to regain my physical strength and to relearn some of the very basic skills I'd lost, like how to feed and dress myself."

When he was pushing himself to the limits, Fred's will to live intensified. But a few others in the hospital gave up and even committed suicide. "I don't know if I ever seriously thought about ending it all . . . That didn't hold much weight for me."

When he left rehab in 1966, Fred was anything but a broken man. Although his body was messed up badly, his mind was teeming with ideas. Once again he began to reach out for his dreams. "I wanted to do what I had thought about all my life. I used to read adventure books as a little kid. I wanted to bicycle around the world, trek the Rocky Mountains, travel the Pan American Highway from Alaska to the southern tip of South America. I wanted all of that action I could get."

Fred was bubbling with a positive attitude. Unlike many who are down on themselves, he wanted to reach new heights and was willing to do whatever was required.

In 1981, the "International Year of Disabled Persons," Fred and his intrepid crew were making headlines around the world. The adventurers were crossing the United States from coast to coast—in *wheelchairs!* The dangerous trip had begun in Fred's mind. "I was really looking for a way to go across America on bicycle or the closest thing to it. I don't know why that appealed to me, but it did." Fred had been involved in marathon races and the development of racing wheelchairs. But one day he thought to himself, *A guy in a wheelchair could probably push across America. Let's get after it.*

For over a year, Fred's house in Florida was wallpapered with maps of every state through which his wheelchair caravan would roll. His phone bill was out of sight, but the trip was coming together.

For 155 days, Fred and his crew traveled, what he claims, are the most perilous pieces of real estate in the world. In his book, *The Continental Quest,* Fred wrote that he knew "the road of life was going to be tough on the best of days. It was going to be miserable on average days. And it promised to be fatal on a bad day."

Fred's predictions weren't off base. What started as a dream turned into a most strenuous—yet worthwhile—adventure for Fred and his crew members. But Fred didn't stop there.

Not satisfied with crossing the United States at ten miles per hour in a wheelchair, Fred is dreaming of another adventure shaping up as this is being written: "The Amazon Quest," a taxing challenge for any human being. Before you shake your head and exclaim, "This guy's crazy—it's just a pipe dream," remember that Fred isn't a talker. He's a doer who lives for his dreams and is willing to sacrifice the time and energy to make them a reality.

"The Amazon Quest"

Imagine it: Ten disabled American and Brazilian adventurers boating down the Amazon River, the largest, most treacherous river in the world. It is a twenty-two-hundred-mile quest into the unknown described by Fred as "an exploration into human geography—an examination of limits, real and imagined, an expression of mankind's spiritual resilience, a journey of the spirit." Still in his planning stages, Fred thinks affirmatively: "Maybe that's the difference between a dream and a vision. This dream has weight and is being carried along with its own force."

After my first interview with Fred, I met with a group of business people at a service club. I spoke about "The Amazon Quest" and the man behind this magnificent venture. Following my talk, one of the members, who is able-bodied, related his dream: "I've always wanted to travel to Europe and Asia and see the great wonders of the world I have read about for years. And after the trip write a book of travel tips about the places I had visited. But when and where would I find the time to do it? I know it's only wishful thinking.

"With my job and the financial and social responsibilities I have, there's no way I have any time for much outside of my job, let alone any time left for writing a book that might never be accepted by a publisher. I guess I'll just check out the books at the library and read about the Great Wall of China and the ruins of Athens. What else can I do?"

While I was listening to the man's admission, I thought how Margaret Mitchell wrote the epic novel *Gone with the Wind*. While she was still employed full-time at an Atlanta newspaper, she penned it bit by bit. Mitchell found time because she was committed to finishing the book, regardless of the sweat. Of course, she had no assurance that a publisher would accept it. But it was her "possible dream."

Like Mitchell, Fred McBee was willing to dare and to dream. He now teaches college courses at the University of South Florida and participates in scores of athletic tournaments, and still has time to plan new adventures. So, what keeps him going? "I don't want my disability to rob me of these experiences. After all, when it's all over, all you have left is your experiences. I believe life itself is a quest. So, I will always have something out there in the works because I have no shortage of ideas about what to do. The problem is getting it done and making the adaptations to see that it happens —and that it is rewarding. But that's the challenge of achievement."

Although many of his ventures have been successful, Fred has had his share of failures. What really keeps him going are the scoffers who delight in saying, "You failed, Fred. I guess it can't be done." Fred is not bothered. "I love the 'I-can't-do-it' people. I think they're highly motivational. When someone says, 'I can't do it,' those words push me to show what they really are. 'I can't' is an illusion. There's always a way."

But there's something Fred can't do—he can't perspire (plain old sweat). This dysfunction is a result of the paralysis. That in itself could prevent making trips to locales like the Amazon, where the average temperature is often over 100 degrees. Fred spells it out: "I do take the dangers very seriously. I recognize it is a risk, and I've met it before in the Mohave Desert and other places where I've been in the heat for a long period of time. What I'll probably do in the Amazon is what I've done before—use a 'Cool Head' (a cooling vest and headgear worn by astronauts). It circulates cool fluid around your chest and head. The bottom line is this: If you recognize the risk, it's a challenge to work around it."

One of Fred's crew members on The Amazon Quest is Robert Hardin, also in this book (Chapter 6). Robert affirms that Fred has an "indomitable spirit." "After you're injured," Fred said, "there comes a point when you say, 'I've got that left.' I've got my spirit and my soul left. They are mine and are as good as ever, maybe stronger, because they're fire-tested. I see the 'indomitable spirit' all the time in my community."

Fred is hoping to make his trip down the Amazon as soon as he finds financial banking. The team will fly to Manaus, Brazil, where they will be taken to a 110-foot-long government boat, compliments of the governor of the state of Amazon. The boat will carry them upriver to the Brazil-Peru border. Along the way the crew will meet with members of Brazil's disabled community and present them with 100 wheelchairs as a gesture of friendship.

After the trip is completed, the ship will be used as a cruising hospital. Aside from the sheer dynamics of the Quest, the expedition will hopefully create a legacy of goodwill throughout Latin America and the world—not a bad achievement for a man who happens to be a quadriplegic. But, then again, Fred McBee is not your average man.

When we parted company, Fred left me with a quote which sums up his life: "The difference between a wise man and an ordinary man is that an ordinary man sees everything as a blessing or a curse while a wise man sees everything as a challenge."

18
Strength:
Betty Everett

"The whole world I was used to had crumbled. There had been no notice or warning. It just died, and I thought I should die with it."

Betty Everett

Photo by David Rogers

Man, this package must have tremendous value, I convinced myself. It was shipped overnight express, and the dark hand-stamped letters riveted my attention: PERSONAL AND CONFIDENTIAL. *Wow, maybe I've won the Reader's Digest Sweepstakes!*

I was in suspense as I ripped open the package. My heart sank within me. My valuable package was stuffed with a brochure and a letter from a West Coast firm publicizing hair transplants. They wanted me to do a feature about their services.

You would be amazed at the number of letters, packages, and other publicity gimmicks a radio or television news department receives in the mail every day of the week. Many of them promote covering up or uncovering what we want or don't want.

We are in the "plastic surgery" phase of life. It's "in." Plastic surgery is hot business, and middle- and upper-class Americans are buying the package. "Tummy tucks" have increased 55 percent since 1984; facelifts, 20 percent; liposuctions (where the fat is sucked out of body tissues) have boomed nearly 80 percent in the last two years, becoming the most popular cosmetic surgery of all.

Plastic surgeons are writing and lecturing, and it is paying off with lots of business. Breast reductions or enlargements and wrinkle deletions are available to those with the money. The watchword seems to have become, "If you don't like something, get rid of it." Sometimes people can actually endanger themselves. How many of us want the "perfect tan"? Dermatologists continually warn us of the dangers of too much sun and ultraviolet rays, but how many sun worshippers are listening?

We are in an age of fantastic surgical and technological breakthroughs, but as many are discovering for themselves, surgery won't radically affect one's self-image. The outer layer can be dramatically transformed in several hours, but the person still remains the same beneath the surface.

"I Want to Kill Myself!"

Many celebrities, with the world seemingly at their feet, have tried suicide. Quite a number have succeeded. One after another prominent entertainers have either deliberately or unwittingly killed themselves with drugs and/or alcohol. They had it made . . . or did they?

Suicides are occurring in epidemic proportions. Some estimates claim there is one every five minutes. Other figures are more drastic. Anxiety and depression contribute significantly to suicide.

According to a 1987 Lou Harris survey, "nearly 2.5 million Americans may be hooked on benzodiazepines. Six million adults in the U.S. have been taking tranquilizers on a constant basis for more than one year." It has been estimated that up to 40 percent of those using these drugs for more than six months may have withdrawal symptoms when they try to quit. In 1987, eight of the major twenty drugs which sent people to hospital emergency rooms for drug-abuse reactions were benzodiazepines.

There is a direct link between drug use and the anxiety which more and more young people and adults are facing. The pressure to belong, to achieve, to "make it," to conform, ad infinitum, is creating an anxiety-ridden society.

Perhaps our culture is too strung out on "the beautiful people," with so many of us wanting to be a part of the "glamour generation." Randy Palmer wrote in the *Presbyterian Journal:*

> Most of us are preoccupied with celebrity and drama, interested in form more than substance. We see Reggie Jackson or Cheryl Tiegs, or Senator Kennedy or John Travolta on TV or magazine covers, and we say to ourselves, *He is somebody,* with the obvious, if unspoken implication of that quote, "I am nobody."

When we are sold on the glitzy package of beauty, popularity, and acceptance, we are setting ourselves up for destruction.

"I'm Dreaming!"

Betty Everett had an enjoyable life-style. She had security—a fulfilling career as a teacher, a successful husband, high social standing in the elite circles of the community, and material possessions. Betty was a "shaker and mover." Politicians sought her advice. Invitations to the most elegant parties were never in short supply. Everything was going her way. She relished the attention and prestige. Betty was on top of the world, and nothing could destroy the life she savored . . . until . . .

October 25, 1982: Betty awoke from a restful sleep. But what was wrong? There was total silence in the room. "Something awful was happening, but I didn't know what it was," she told me. "But I was scared, really scared."

When she opened her mouth, she couldn't hear the words she was speaking. "Oh, dear Lord," she cried, "it can't be. I can't hear!" Betty was deaf! And she lost her speech control two weeks later. The doctors labeled her disorder "auto-immunity," or a failure of the immune system. It meant a 92 percent hearing loss.

In less than eighteen months, the community leader lost her job, her friends, and her husband! *I'm dreaming,* she kept thinking to herself. *It can't be real.* But it was. Her world was shattered—tossed up into the air like confetti, only to be swept away by the street cleaners.

"My marriage ended the day I couldn't hear. My husband couldn't deal with it and wasn't willing to learn how to handle my deafness. Of course, I didn't know how to handle it myself."

After the divorce, Betty wanted to escape, so she moved in with her mother. Her friends of high standing didn't drop by. "Unlike other handicaps, my problem didn't generate a warm response from the people I considered friends. The inability to communicate and let them know I was hurting, at first was too much to accept and to explain to them. It was impossible for me to teach them to communicate with me because I just didn't know how."

It was a catastrophe! Betty had gone from the mountaintop to the bottom of the valley in only a few months. The losses were crushing. "The whole world I was used to had crumbled. There had been no notice or warning. It just died, and I thought I should die with it. My so-called successful marriage had gone to pot. My teaching job went down the tubes because I couldn't talk to the kids, and I couldn't hear them. My own son wasn't able to relate to his mother. The loneliness of not being able to hear him say 'I love you, Mom' was enough to sink me into a deep, deep depression."

Betty tried desperately to crawl out of her shell, but the inability to communicate sent her scurrying back home. "I couldn't even go to movies, churches, or parties. Everything I once took for granted was gone. When I went to church, I couldn't hear what the minister was saying or enjoy the music. I couldn't handle walking into the service and not know what was going on. I came out angrier than when I went in. That was a real loss since church was a factor in my life."

Especially frustrating to her was being in a room with a crowd of people during a party and feeling as if she were all alone. All around her, people were laughing and talking, but she couldn't hear them—and they couldn't understand her. She would sit by herself and cry on the inside.

"Try going out for a candlelight dinner if you can't hear and your date can. It's impossible. There's not enough light to read the lips of the person with you. I know from being in that situation."

Betty still had her son. "But," as she shared, "I felt like a burden to him. Here was a sixteen-year-old boy who had to treat his mom differently. Most kids can yell, 'Hey, Mom, where are my socks?' He had to learn to come to me and ask me face-to-face so I could read his lips. I wanted virtually to find a gun and kill myself."

What stopped her?

"Believe me, it would have been much easier to commit suicide or to withdraw from society and live in a little room and say, 'OK, Social Security and welfare, you take care of me.' But a little voice down inside said, 'Not yet. All isn't lost. You can do more than this. You don't have to give in to it.' The inner strength or spirituality kept me alive. It had to, since I couldn't make a decision by myself at that point in my life. Oftentimes, death seemed pretty nice to me, but I finally chose to live. When I did, I prayed, 'OK, God, if I go on, let's make this a positive situation.' When I made that decision, things seemed to open up for me. It's because my goals were off of the deafness and onto the living."

"I Want to Live!"

After three months at her mother's home, Betty grew tired of hiding from the reality of her disability. Her doctors made it plain: "Betty, there's nothing we can do to restore your hearing. You have a choice to make. Either feel sorry for yourself or learn how to lip-read."

Betty spent the next nine months in lip-reading classes. She then attended Tennessee State University working on a master's degree in counseling. While she was there, Betty was challenged by a friend to confront her hearing problem. For the first time since the deafness began, she came to terms with her denial of the disability. As she later admitted, "I wasn't coping with the pain, frustration, and anger. I wasn't letting myself go through the grieving process. There were days when I just cried and didn't want anyone to know about my pain. I tried to put on this phony image of tackling the handicap and acted like I didn't have a physical disability. The most important concept of becoming a fully functional person was to reach out and tell people that I was needing help and that I was hurting badly."

Once she was willing to share her private feelings, Betty accepted the risk of being insulted and even rejected. "Every day I'm with people is a risk because, when I say, 'I'm hearing impaired and need to read your lips,' that means I'm giving some obligation to the other person. I'm saying, 'I need you to do something in order for us to communicate.' That person can give only one of two answers . . . yes or no. It's a fragile situation at first, but it's worth the risk."

After she earned a master's degree in counseling, Betty pounded on doors trying to find a school or institution that would hire a deaf person with sixteen years of teaching experience. The answer became predictable: "I'm sorry, Ms. Everett, but we have a more qualified prospect." Rejection, for whatever the reason, always hurts.

"People used to call me and ask my opinions about world trends for the next ten years. That was before I lost my hearing. My disability obviously outweighed a degree and years of teaching experience."

Betty could have fled and hidden in her mother's home. But this time she was downright angry. *If I give in to rejection, I lose,* she lectured herself, *and I won't do that anymore. If I can't get a job the normal way, I'll be a little crafty about it.*

Instead of knocking on more doors for work, Betty walked into the Oasis Center, a shelter for economically disadvantaged youths. She refused a job application. She wanted to demonstrate her skills up front. "I can't make it on the kind of money you might offer me now. Give me a chance as a full-time volunteer." Betty was determined to stick it out and wait for an offer worth accepting. Her plan worked!

"Shortly after the interview, a job opportunity was available. I applied and got the position. After six months, I was promoted to a coordinator and youth employment counselor," Betty joyfully concluded. She was later named program director.

Betty's story isn't a Pollyanna saga that can be summarized in several pages and then concluded with a happy ending. That wouldn't be accurate. A year after I met her, Betty told me she has confidence in herself and her abilities. But, in her own words, "I'm still very much in the grieving process, and I'm not afraid to admit it."

Betty wants to straighten out what she considers misinformation. She feels some "experts" aren't being on the level with the public. Many of the books about the grieving process categorize each stage and expect the people who have experienced a loss to run through those stages from A to Z.

Betty feels those expectations are not fair. "None of us can systematically go through the grieving process one step to the next step without missing a beat. Something can trigger an emotion in us, and we can bounce back. You can be in two stages at one time and then reverse stages. It's not a neat little bundle that can be handled in a specific way or time."

While I was putting together this chapter, there was a news flash about a presidential candidate who declared he had never been depressed. A political expert responded with: "It's unfortunate that a politician has a better chance of being elected if he denies ever seeing a psychologist or counselor for emotional problems. If he were honest about them, his career would be in jeopardy."

Betty is not surprised. She feels it's time we drop the "macho" image of expecting emotional perfectionism. "What's wrong with admitting pain?" she asks. "American society is moving along intellectually and analytically. But what I'm finding as a counselor and a disabled person is: the emotional aspect is not developed at all. That's why people like me are off kilter when we experience pain in the grieving process. All of a sudden, we want to stop and analyze it. That's a bunch of rubbish! Allow yourself to feel the pain. Don't run or hide from it, and don't feel ashamed. If we can only allow ourselves to experience the pain, we are able to remain in balance. I think our society is, very simply, scared of tears."

Betty isn't invited to the same gatherings or mentioned in the social gossip columns anymore. But she's still a "shaker and mover." Only this time, Betty is molding the lives of kids who need guidance and support. As she says with dignity, "I'm an advocate for people who are not willing, able, or capable of expressing what their needs are. In my work with disadvantaged youths, if I make a difference in one kid's life, I've been a genuine shaker and mover."

Betty Everett no longer hides. She is touching young lives with compassion and strength as few can. Because of her pain, she can understand the pain suffered by others. Now this strong-willed woman can hug a confused, teary-eyed youngster and say, "It's all right to hurt. I've been there, too." In her case the message is going through every day.

Part V:
The Believers

19
Resilience:
Lottie Fortune

"I was being treated like a menopausal old woman. . . . I felt older and worse by the day. My teeth felt like falling out, and my stomach hurt all the time."

Lottie Fortune

Photo Courtesy Lottie Fortune

When my interview with Lottie Fortune first aired, the phone response was unbelievable. "Is there any way you could tell us what this woman did to cure her arthritis?" was the typical question. Lottie had battled the crippling disability and pain nearly a decade ago—and now was enjoying life free from arthritis.

It was not surprising her story had generated such a positive reaction. Over thirty-seven million Americans suffer from one form of arthritis or another. That averages out to one person in every three families. Many have lost hope and have given up on life and themselves.

But Lottie was not among them. She is a vibrant sixty-year-old who plays tennis three times a week, has earned a yellow belt in karate, and has led support groups on arthritis.

Only eight years before we met, Lottie couldn't bend over the sink to brush her teeth. Climbing in and out of the car became a horrifying ordeal. Merely holding onto a wooden spoon or rolling pin was painful, and a good night's sleep was nonexistent. Lottie, then living in Boston, had been diagnosed with osteoarthritis.

The doctors laid it on the line to her. "Lottie, there's nothing you can do about the disease. You'll simply have to accept it."

"But," the determined woman demanded, "there has to be something I can do. I can't live my life in constant pain and not do anything about it."

"There are ways to handle the pain," they advised her. "We can prescribe medications that will alleviate part of the hurt, but that's about it."

Lottie wouldn't face the "facts." At first, she was in denial and thought to herself, *This couldn't be happening to me. I was following all the good health rules, or thought I was.* When the pain became unbearable, she had to accept the reality of the diagnosis.

But Lottie was not allowing anyone, including her physicians, to assume control of her life. Then and there she made a pact with herself to become responsible for overcoming the arthritic pain. Lottie first and foremost prayed: "Dear God, please help me find a way to end this disease. I need Your guidance, Lord. I want to live—not merely exist."

While she was praying and hoping, Lottie tried to be, in her own words, a "good patient." She did what the doctors asked her to do and would not complain. She was also swallowing dozens of prescribed pills daily. Starting with twelve aspirin a day, she was popping all kinds of anti-inflammatory drugs into her system—like Indocin, Nalfon, cortisone, and more. But the joint-wrenching pain persisted, and not long afterward, side-effects from the medications were spreading like an oil slick on water.

"I was being treated like a chronic, menopausal old woman," she angrily told me. "And I felt older and worse by the day. My teeth felt like falling out, and my stomach hurt all the time. My hands started to bleed from the fingertips, and canker sores were burning like wildfire in my mouth. Sleeping was impossible. I'd be up several times during the night, hoping for daylight. Just lying down on the bed was painful. I'd get up cautiously, and I was very stiff. The pain would course up my back and down my legs. The medication didn't help me perform tasks that most people take for granted. Getting in and out of a car was virtually impossible. I'd have to lift my leg up to get in. Sitting in the backseat was impossible. I would rather have been put on top of the car and strapped on."

Lottie, like the majority of arthritis patients, had no idea about what else she could do. So she made more trips to the specialists. *Just maybe,* she was fondly hoping, *they'll have a new medication that will help me.*

"Please, Doctor," she would tell one doctor after another, "there must be something I can do. I have so many dreams and things I want to do, but now my life is so painful. I want to rid myself of this disease."

The pleas were invariably answered the same. "Lottie, you'll have to take your medicine and cope with the disease the best you can. There aren't any 'miracle cures.' You'd better accept what you have as your new way of life. Don't fight it. You'll just be disappointed."

Lottie was tired of being "a good patient." She was gradually, but surely, becoming disenchanted with the medical advice she was receiving. Like millions of other arthritics, she was willing to try anything. "I was hurting so much, even a faint promise of a cure would have been enough to make me go for it," the dynamic woman recollects.

"I saw a psychiatrist and was hypnotized. That didn't work. I was at the end of my rope, and anything was worth a try, even copper bracelets and apricot pits. I knew some people with cancer who had tried the pits, and thought maybe they'd work for me." Nothing did. She reached the point where she read everything she could about the disease. For the most part, the material advised: see your doctor, take your medication, rest, and exercise. She did—and was still miserable.

Lottie's condition was rapidly deteriorating. The pain in her joints was torturous. *Maybe,* she convinced herself after a doctor's suggestion, *I'll need to have a hip fusion.* She checked that out with a rheumatologist and an orthopedic surgeon. "I figured it was the last alternative left. I was scared and depressed and grew tired of sitting in doctor's offices. I had to deal with the pain soon."

Before following through with surgery, Lottie painfully drove to downtown Boston in search of more literature. Any book about arthritis was an easy sale for the desperate woman. She had read dozens of them but had found nothing to reverse the disease.

"Please, Lord, this time show me a book that will remove this terrible pain," she silently prayed. Still clinging to the slightest inkling of a miracle, Lottie spotted a book store and mused, *I've got nothing to lose by going in and browsing.*

While sifting through the shelves, she spotted an arthritis cookbook by a Chinese doctor, *The Arthritic's Cookbook* by Dr. Collin H. Dong. She casually picked it up and became totally absorbed in it. "As I read it, I found the story was so similar to mine that I could have written the book myself. Dr. Dong had gone through the same pain, but he was only thirty years old when it was happening to him. But at fifty years old I had a little bit more aging under my belt. Before a clerk noticed me and would probably tease me about reading the whole book in the store, I had to buy it.

"The book was an answer to my prayers," Lottie happily declared. "I had eaten healthy foods but had never stuck to a daily diet without meats and dairy products."

Lottie was enthralled by the book and the diet. "I was filled with hope again. 'Oh, please, Lord, let this work,' I prayed again and again. I couldn't believe my body. After the first week, 50 percent of the pain was gone. I was able to sleep and to go up and down steps in my house. I was bending over to brush my teeth without holding onto my back. I simply knelt down and thanked the good Lord. After the second week, I lost all the pain. It was gone! I felt this was a miracle.

"I became convinced the food I had been eating wasn't very good for me, such as the meats and dairy products. I thought an older person like myself needed plenty of calcium. So, I had devoured cheeses and milk. As I increased my calcium intake, I read about milk being a big problem with arthritics. Then I began to get my calcium from fresh vegetables like broccoli. I infrequently take calcium tablets because I do suffer a few cramps in my legs if I'm lacking the vitamin."

Her incessant quest to overcome the disease paid off for Lottie. It was time to celebrate and thank God for being with her. "God had answered my prayers. He had directed me to the book and had provided the support I needed at that time in my life. I had been physically at rock bottom. I had been almost completely without energy. I had been a living body of pain, but that part of my life was history."

Lottie's prayers were answered, but she was also willing to discipline herself toward overcoming the arthritis. In other words, Lottie accepted the responsibility for her good health. She had to cooperate with Divine Providence, and no doctor or counselor could have accomplished what she did by herself.

Lottie became her own diet specialist. She even devised a special diet that is suited to her needs. Unlike *The Arthritic's Cookbook,* she included some fruits and eliminated others, such as oranges, grapefruit, and lemons.

"I had become a health faddist. I used to laugh at people who were into health foods, but I don't laugh anymore. I'm living a wonderful life because of what I eat and don't eat."

But Lottie's success story wasn't popular with some. One of her doctors gave her a lecture when she shared the good news with him. "He kept talking about quacks and never spoke one word about the diet. He thought I was probably 'in remission,' but I wanted to tell him the doctor who wrote the book had been in remission for thirty years."

Lottie and her husband left Boston in 1980 and moved to Hendersonville, Tennessee. She wanted to help others battle their disease. That is exactly what she has done and is doing. Lottie formed two support groups.

"I want to show you something," Lottie told the new members. "You may not believe this. But I have gone through what many of you are feeling right now."

As she pulls the vials of pills and medication from her pockets, the audience is glued to her every word. "I used to take all these pills—and more. I used to wear a cast because my fingers were getting stiff at night, but I don't anymore."

Then Lottie lays it on the line, driving home the fact that each person is responsible for his own health, not a doctor or a hospital. "I am responsible for my health; you are responsible for yours," Lottie veritably preaches to her support groups. "Nobody knows my body as well as I do. If we listen to our bodies very carefully, they tell us an awful lot. I love sweets and don't think a meal is complete without a cookie or a dessert. But when I eat a candy bar," she laughs, "it will go straight to my knees, and I'll hurt—and know it's not good for me. It's important to listen and pay attention to your body."

Lottie makes sure her listeners understand that the diet is not a guarantee and will not help every person who tries it. She shares her experiences and expects her regimen to work for some of her support group members. She humbly admits, "I can't and won't say I'm completely cured. I've reversed a serious, painful illness. Having a positive attitude and having faith and the hope that I would recover helped bring about what I believe was a miracle."

Many of her support-group members have reported consider-
able progress.

"After only four sessions," Lottie eagerly reports, "a thirty-
year-old mother of two has become a different person. The arthritis was so bad she had her arm in a cast. Rheumatoid arthritis had
taken hold all over her body. A change in diet and an exercise
program have paid dividends. Her brace is off, and she's free of
pain. Her cheeks are even pink again, and she's lost weight."

As we were wrapping up the interview, Lottie wanted to talk
about what she and her husband had in store for themselves over
the weekend. "We're going white-water rafting. We've never done
that before," she enthusiastically remarked. "I couldn't have done
that back in Boston. I wouldn't have been able to get into the raft,
let alone hang onto the oar."

One cannot believe Lottie Fortune will ever have another bout
with arthritis—but somehow if she does, she will remember the
years she has lived without its discomfort and pain. This active,
painless period has afforded her a whole new perspective about
what one can do when "the experts" tell him/her to accept "the
inevitable."

Hers is a hard-to-beat success story. Lottie Fortune indeed
possesses resiliency, which the dictionary defines as: "the capabili-
ty of a strained body to recover in size and shape after deformation
caused especially by compressive stress; an ability to recover from
or adjust easily to misfortune or change." That describes Lottie
to a T!

Suggestions from Lottie's
Modified Arthritis Diet

Special cautions: No red meat, small amounts of milk and cheese,
low-acid fruit and juices, two eggs per week.

Snacks: Yogurt, apples, peaches, bananas, grapes, melons, bran
muffins, banana or zucchini bread, date nut bread, sherbet, al-
monds, sunflower seeds, popcorn, dried fruit, oatmeal or almond
cookie with low-fat milk.

Supplements: Cod-liver oil, Vitamins E, C, B-12, Calcium, Zinc, alfalfa

Party appetizers: Zucchini quiche, salmon spread on crackers, fresh vegetables in yogurt dip, shrimp (but not if you have a cholesterol problem), smoked oysters on crackers

Possible breakfasts: 1. Cranberry juice, scrambled egg, turkey or ham biscuit, black decaf coffee; 2. grape juice, corn or wheat cereal, low-fat milk, decaf coffee; 3. apple juice, hard-boiled egg, bran muffin, decaf; 4. grape, cranberry, or apple juice, toasted bagel or whole wheat roll; 5. one of the juices, two slices of whole wheat bread

Lunches: 1. Salmon, crackers, apple, lo-cal non-cola drink; 2. cottage cheese, peaches or bananas, crackers, water; 3. peanut-butter or cheese crackers, apple, lo-cal non-cola drink; 4. turkey sandwich on rye bread with lettuce, pickle, banana, water; 5. filet of fish sandwich with lettuce, mayonnaise on whole-wheat roll, peach, water

Dinners: 1. Baked potato with non-fat spread, broccoli, carrots, water; 2. baked chicken, rice, peas, carrots, watermelon, water; 3. linguini and clams (garlic, parsley, onions), tossed salad with lo-cal dressing, water; 4. stir-fried chicken and vegetables (peas, onions, mushrooms, peppers, carrots), soy sauce, rice, water; 5. homemade vegetable soup, chicken bullion with peas, carrots, onions, string beans, corn (and leftovers), noodles, water.

*Use salt substitutes and special no-salt vegetable seasonings; also low-cholesterol spread for bread, for cooking, and seasoning; also decaf coffee.
Other dinner entrees: vegetarian pizza: no tomato sauce, very little cheese and plenty of onions, peppers, mushrooms, olives; chicken, turkey, or shrimp gumbo soup (with suggested vegetables above).

20
Humor:
Edgar Allen Poe

"I wish I had had cancer when I was twenty-five years old. I learned how to live and enjoy life after I had it."

Captain Edgar Allen Poe

Photo by Bob Churchwell

"Mr. Dahmen, this is the White House. Could you please hold?" As I held the receiver, all kinds of thoughts raced through my mind. *Could the President be calling? Maybe we're getting an exclusive interview.* How wrong I was!

The woman whose voice I finally heard was from the press liaison office of the White House. I soon found out we were not being offered an interview with our Chief Executive. Rather, the caller curtly told me, "Your reporter Liz White requested the President of the United States to perform a service that is definitely against the very nature of his office."

You can imagine my anxiety! *What could Liz possibly have done to prompt this kind of reaction from the White House? Maybe she forced her way past the Secret Service to get an autograph. Oh no,* I thought, *she'll probably be on the evening newscasts, being hand-cuffed and hustled away. The footage will be shown worldwide on the evening news.* The scenario worsened as my thoughts ran wild.

To make a long story short, Liz had asked the President to read a promo for our Nashville radio station at a White House briefing for Southern journalists. According to the woman from the White House press office, he did exactly that!

"Now I dare say that every radio station in the country will want to have the President read one for them. And we all know presidents don't do that kind of thing!"

I was in a state of shock, but I tried to answer: "Miss, I'm sorry if this disturbs you, but I still don't understand the seriousness of the request. If Mr. Reagan went ahead and read the promo, he must have taken it good naturedly. No one forced him to do it, and after all he is the President and made a quick decision to go ahead and honor Liz's request."

Another call arrived from Washington, and I assured the White House representative I would call her back. The caller identified himself as a writer with the *Washington Post* (I knew for sure it wasn't Woodward or Bernstein, but as the day progressed they probably heard about it. Everyone else in the media did.).

I immediately asked the *Post* man how the President had reacted to Liz's request (passed to him on a slip of paper). Was the

President miffed about it? "Not all all. He chuckled and read the promo—not once but twice. He said it reminded him of his days as an announcer in Iowa."

The writer from the *Post* read the promo to me:

I'm Ronald Reagan. Whenever I'm in Nashville, I listen to Radio 650, WSM, the fifty-thousand-watt blowtorch of the South.

Soon, the station switchboard lines were lit up like a Fourth of July fireworks show. All day long we were besieged with calls from television and radio networks, wire services, newspapers, magazines, and foreign news services. As the day wore on, the questions became more intense and even severe. One of the network reporters told me, "We've had Watergate, Pearlygate, Irangate, and now Promogate."

White House reporters later asked the President about the incident, and he lightheartedly answered, "The young woman asked me to read a promo that every other station would love to have." The President was good natured about it, but some media people thought it had dire consequences for the nation! In my wildest dreams I could not imagine all the hoopla that was being created.

When did we lose our capacity to laugh and to have fun? Even the President has a right to joke when he wants to. In fact, a sense of humor should be one of the prerequisites for being President. One of the best antidotes for stress and depression is finding humor in life. It can heal the sick and mend the wounded.

A hearty laugh can give you a "runner's high," releasing endocrines, the body's natural painkillers. A research study by a Yale University medical team proved that laughter clears the respiratory system, provides a healthy emotional outlet, combats boredom, and gives one a better self-image. Beyond that, a good laugh helps us enjoy life far more than when we frown.

A Lesson from the Captain

I would love to introduce the Washington press corps to a friend of mine, Captain Edgar Allen Poe. As far as he knows, he is not related to the great author. His expertise is on the river. For over forty years he has held sway on tugboats, showboats, and barges, but there is far more to the Captain than his knowledge of the waterways and piloting powerful riverboats.

The Captain is a crusty fellow who also possesses the gentleness and compassion of one of my son's teachers. He has come by his unusual personality the hard way. Several years ago the Captain was diagnosed with a terminal disease.

"Captain Poe," his doctor gloomily predicted, "you don't have more than eighteen months to live. The cancer in your neck is going to kill you."

That kind of bad news even rattled the usually unflappable Captain. He felt as if a lightning bolt had run through his chest. *Why me?* the earthy Captain cried. *I'm not a killer, not a thief.* And he prayed, "Lord, why does it have to be me?"

After the initial shock the Captain made a pact with himself. *No matter how bad it looks or what these doctors tell me,* he etched into his mind, *I will not lose my sense of humor. That's all I've got left. Ain't nobody gonna take that away from me.*

Easier said than done. The Captain had fought adversity in the waters and had always come out the winner. But this time the white-haired pilot was not in control.

Lying around in a hospital bed wasn't his idea of a good time. The routine drove him bonkers. Every morning at five he was awakened. At eight he had breakfast. The rest of the day he was fried with radiation treatments. What affected him the most was what he labeled "my loss of dignity."

"Everything was clinical and dry," he commented. "The nurse would check in with me first thing in the morning and ask me how I was doing, but she never waited for a response. I was probably the twenty-fifth patient she had asked. Seemingly I had become a number on a chart, not a person. No one called me Captain Poe or Poe or anything."

Captain Poe wasn't a vegetable. He was a tough-skinned master pilot who wasn't about to let cancer snatch away his pride. He wanted to live, and that meant standing up for himself, like the time he was strapped to an iron table. The table was stone hard as he lay there shivering in his nightgown, waiting for his radiation treatment. As soon as he was strapped down, the doctors and nurses walked outside to watch an eclipse. That was too much for the fourth-generation riverman.

"What's the matter with you people?" he yelled at the top of his lungs.

But no one was around to hear him. When a nurse came into the room, the Captain pled with her, "Please, I have to get up. I think I've got a cramp in my back."

"No way, Mister," she sharply snapped back.

"Look, Lady . . ." he continued to beg with all the strength he could muster in his condition. "I've got to get up. This table's killing me!"

Tired of hearing him complain, the nurse decided to check his back. "Well, you're right. You do have a cramp."

"Lady," he came back. "I've got cancer. That's why I'm here. I'm not in as a mental case. I know when I'm in pain. If you strap me down one more time, I'm gonna get you if you run off to stare at another eclipse!"

Apparently she caught his drift. The next day, as the doctors and nurses began another radiation treatment on him, the nurse reminded them, "Now, don't strap him down too long, 'cause he'll hit you!"

When he wasn't tangling with the nurses, the Captain was laughing with his fellow patients. Humor was the best approach in coping with the unpredictability of his hospitalization and disease. "The patients," he mused, "can make or break you. Making friends with the person next to you is the first step. But what's even greater is helping that fellow feel better. When you give, you get back. This is true more so when you're sick. If you feel bad and crack a joke, you can overcome about anything. I've found people who didn't have any sense of humor at all until they contracted cancer. After being diagnosed with the illness, they said, 'Look, we've got to laugh at what is reality, and reality at times is funny.' They learn to laugh with life instead of against it."

Captain Poe was amazingly blessed. Surgeons decided to remove the tumor from his neck. When they did, the tumor literally fell out. The cancer was nowhere else in his body! When he awoke from the surgery, his family told him, "The cancer is gone. You're gonna live!"

"You're not telling me the truth," he kept insisting. Several hours later, his family and the doctors had persuaded him the cancer was gone. But Poe was not the same man after the episode that could have destroyed him. "I said right then and there, *Whatever happens to me, I'll never complain again.* It took something like the cancer to shake me up and make me appreciate the things I have in life. Although I'm the first to say, 'Don't take life seriously,' I'm more serious about living life and enjoying it. As many have said, 'Stop and smell the roses.' Believe me, I don't take the simple things for granted anymore."

Since his bout with cancer a few years ago, the Captain has become sort of a folk hero in the South. As the Captain of the *General Jackson Showboat* in Nashville, he's an occasional guest on the Nashville Network's "Nashville Now" show. His stories, even the few "inside" river jokes he can tell on the air, are familiar to millions of television viewers. The celebrity status, though, hasn't erased the memories of his scrap with cancer. They have given him what he has today—a sense of what's really important in life.

"I wish I had had cancer when I was twenty-five years old. I learned how to live and enjoy life after I had it. I don't care what happens to me today. I had my apartment broken into, and everything was stolen. People said, 'How can you joke about it?' I tell them, 'Hey, it happened, and I might as well make the best of it.' There's got to be a silver lining somewhere. I woke up that morning and had no underwear. It's funny. Life goes on. The next week, my pickup truck was stolen. Well, so what? I got to meet the sheriff in Franklin, and he's a fine fellow. That was the good side of it."

As the Captain's hands skillfully guide the *General Jackson* wheel, tourists surround the pilot house. Many of them wave at the smiling gentleman dressed in his spotless uniform. Others are snapping pictures of him, and they will carry memories of a cruise down the Cumberland River and a Captain who appears to be a character straight out of a Mark Twain novel.

But the image is different from the man in charge of the fifteen-hundred-ton vessel. He's not a fictional character but someone who could have been destroyed by a terminal illness.

"If you have the right attitude, you can whip almost any problem. I know it sounds mystical, but there's too much proof that attitude and laughter can overcome mental and physical ailments. What I don't understand is: we all have this evidence that stress can cause so many ailments. But nobody uses the flip side of that—if you fight stress and don't let it throw you, nothing can get you down. Just keep this in mind. Less than 6 percent of the people in the world are fortunate enough to be born in America. There's blessing number one you have to be thankful for. That should be more than enough incentive to straighten out a bad attitude."

As I left the boat, Captain Poe grinned and gave me a message for my reporter, Liz White. "Tell her I think it's great what she had the President do. It's about time we stop taking everything so seriously and have a good time, even if it's with the man in the White House."

I kind of expected that from a man who was given only eighteen months to live and is still around years later to laugh about it.

21
Courage:
O. B. McClinton

"The instant my kidneys were blocked off, my body stopped acting like it had since I was born. I had taken it for granted. I should have been saying all those years, 'Thank God, I am blessed.'"

O. B. McClinton

Photo Courtesy Sunbird Records and
Tessier Talent, Inc., Nashville

After months of typing manuscript chapters and interviewing dozens of prospective subjects, I was burned out. I couldn't touch another typewriter key, and just thinking about sitting down and writing another story was enough to keep me away from my desk. Although I had thrived on the "I Love Life" concept, I was aching for a break.

As I was taking a breather from "I Love Life," I was invited to speak before a small group of women. At the time I was reluctant to accept the invitation, but I simply could not say no. "We would love to hear a newsman talk about his search for the good news," the group's program director persuaded me. When I met with them on a Saturday afternoon, I needed a boost myself. Although I explained the "I Love Life" concept and how it started, I was merely mouthing the words and was devoid of enthusiasm.

After the program was over, I thanked the women for the invitation. Before leaving the room, one of the members introduced herself to me. "Jerry, I want you to have this short poem. It's our gift to you. If you believe in what you're doing, I know this will help you," she emphasized.

I thanked her and promised I would read it as soon as I reached home. Instead of dashing to my desk, I plopped onto the couch. "Maybe I'll escape for several hours watching a movie."

While squinting at the summer reruns, I noticed the poem I had laid on the coffee table. I glanced at the words and then became glued to the message of the poem entitled "Believe in Yourself." I knew the words were aimed at me.

> Believe in yourself
> and in your dream
> though impossible things may seem.
> Someday, somehow you'll get through
> to the goal you have in view.
> Mountains fall and seas divide
> before the one who in his stride
> takes a hard road day by day,

sweeping obstacles away.

Believe in yourself and in your plan.
Say not "I cannot," but "I can."
The prizes of life we fail to win
because we doubt the power within.

I had stopped believing in "I Love Life." Instead of saying "I can," I was turning away from my dream. *If I stop now, I thought, my dream dies, and so does the project. Sure, I'm worn out, but that can't be permanent. I won't allow myself to quit. If I give up, I'm to blame and no one else.*

The following day a lovable sports hero, Dick Howser, died. The man who earned cheers as manager of the 1985 World Series Champions, the Kansas City Royals, passed away at the relatively young age of fifty-one. Hearing about his death reminded me of the poem's admonition: "Believe in yourself and in your plan. Say not I cannot, but I can." Dick Howser might well have written those words. He achieved fame as a major-league baseball player and manager. But that was only one facet of his life. Dick's battle to conquer brain cancer was even more overpowering.

One of his players described his fight with cancer like this: "Never in his life did anybody ever question his courage. He fought to beat cancer the same way he fought to win games."

After three operations for a malignant tumor on his brain, Dick still believed in himself and his plan. Only months before his death, he had enthusiastically greeted his players at spring training. His plan was to be there in spite of his illness. Even cancer could not snatch away the excitement of being with his team.

Dick didn't fold up and pray, "OK, God, take me now. This is it." No! He had fame, money, influence, prestige, but all of that could not compare with his love for baseball. That was his mission, and he wasn't ready to give in. His struggle to live wasn't easy, but to him it was worth all the effort.

Dick called to mind, "Believe in yourself and in your dream." Here I was doubting the value of a book I wanted to write—and was about to dump it. The more I concentrated on Dick and the poem, the more I recognized the importance of finishing what I had begun. Many of us give up too easily. I had cried "uncle" many times before . . . but not on "I Love Life," I decided.

When I again sat in front of the typewriter, I made up my mind. *If Dick Howser, with a malignant brain tumor, could meet his players at spring training, I am not about to talk myself out of this dream. I have more interviews and stories to do.*

As Dick Howser dreamed of winning another World Series, I kept alive my vision of doing this book. In the process I thought about another man with a vision, who had his own personal mission and plan in life.

Man with a Mission

At the office I was jotting down ideas for a news series. I heard an energetic voice outside the door.

"Good morning, everyone," the slender black man projected. It was impossible to ignore him as he sat down and chatted with our station's music director. "I got myself a fantastic album that I know is going to be a winner," he exclaimed.

As he was talking, I asked one of the announcers about the intense guy (I thought he was a high-powered record promoter). "No, he doesn't work for a record company," I was informed. "That's O. B. McClinton, the country singer. He really believes in his songs. It's too bad, but O. B. may not be around much longer."

O. B., he told me, had terminal cancer. That surprised me. At that moment, I learned, he had tubes sticking out of his body because of kidney failure. Even though cancer was eating away at his organs, he wasn't lying in bed waiting for death.

Instead, as a singer-songwriter, he was going full tilt writing, recording, and promoting the songs that had built up in him. While he was in the recording studio, his producer said, O. B. "danced so much he had some bleeding the next day."

Once the songs were put onto records and tapes, the work was only begun. O. B. wanted to promote his own music. The native Mississippian hurried around Nashville, plugging the album to

those who would listen to him. O. B. believed in himself. "Ain't
nobody and no disease gonna stop me now," he constantly testified. "God gives me this talent, and I won't stop until He says
it's time to go."

O. B. had driven himself hard through the years. As a youngster
in a small Mississippi town, he knew what had to be done. When
O. B.'s mother had caught him standing on a soft drink case and
drinking from a water fountain, she grabbed him and spanked him
with all her might.

As they walked back home, she scolded him, "O. B., don't you
ever do that again! You broke the white man's law. That fountain's
not for us. It's for whites only."

But that's not right, O. B. thought. *I don't want to be scared of
someone hurting me because I want to drink from a town fountain.*

In many respects, O. B.'s future was decided that day. He
wanted to be loved and to prove to people that he was, in his own
words, "at least worthy of a drink of water."

From then on, the boy with a vibrant smile wrote songs about
people and "characters" in the country neighborhoods where he
lived. When he entertained, everyone responded. "You got talent,
kid. You keep that up, and you'll be a big-name singer some day,"
he was repeatedly told.

Years later, O. B. was writing, recording, and entertaining.
Perhaps he never became a "superstar" recording artist, but O. B.
did what he wanted to do. Since the early 1970s, he had been on
the road, loving every minute of it. "No one is ever gonna take
away what God has given me," he said confidently. Of course, he
didn't expect the onset of a killer disease.

While on a concert tour, O. B. experienced excruciating ab-
dominal pain. When doctors operated on him for appendicitis,
they found a malignant, inoperable tumor.

"O. B.," they quietly announced as he was coming out of the
anesthetic, "it wasn't what we thought. You have terminal cancer."

The moment he heard the bad news, O. B. took a deep breath
and prayed to his Lord. Only God could grant him the power to

keep on going. "Without His help," O. B. confided, "I'd probably jump into the Cumberland River or buy a thirty-eight-caliber revolver and shoot myself. Without God, I wouldn't have been able to face everyday life. But He gave me the equipment to handle it. I'll admit there have been some moments when I was confused and shocked. I thought about my family and not seeing my kids grow up and not performing anymore. Then I started to think differently."

A Beautiful Philosophy

Seldom have I been touched as I was when O. B. candidly revealed his feelings about his life and upcoming death. "The way I deal with my illness is: God is saying: 'O. B., I've always liked you, and you did all the things you were supposed to do. You worked so hard and fast. Everything is done. But now I have trouble up here and have an opening in the Heavenly Choir and need you in it."

Once he was released from the hospital, O. B. moved into action. If his time was short here, he had to do whatever was necessary to leave behind all God had given him. He convinced himself to "find the energy within me to get everything out of me that I'm supposed to leave behind." "Believe in yourself and in your plan" came back to me as O. B. spoke of his mission here and his preparation to meet his Lord.

"I know what God's going to tell me if I don't get the job done. 'It was your job to let others get the strength and happiness from your music, but you messed around and didn't do it.' I still have more songs to sing and intend to record them. I don't want to carry any music with me."

Several of O. B.'s friend urged him to seek special treatments that might somehow cure him of the cancer. He never even tried, "That," he stressed, "is going against my faith and belief in God. If my life is prolonged, the Heavenly Father is the one who should do it. This is my decision, and I plan to stick with it."

O. B. McClinton died September 23, 1987, at a medical center in Nashville. He was forty-seven. When I heard the news, I remembered his visit to the radio station several months before, when we had talked over an hour about his life and career. The excitement in his voice had been contagious. "I'll tell you this," as he opened his shirt and pointed to the tubes inserted into his midsection, "one of the first things we all do after getting out of bed in the morning is go to the bathroom. But I'll bet most of us never give it a second thought. What we should be saying is this: 'Thank you, Lord, for the health I have.'"

"The instant my kidneys were blocked off, my body stopped acting like it had since I was born. I had taken that for granted. I should have been saying all those years, 'Thank You, God, I am blessed. Praise You, Lord.' But I didn't. I was so worried about the external world, trying to make hit records and not the ones I really thought were good."

After that interview, O. B. had dashed off to another radio station. There was no outward indication he had even the slightest idea he was about to die.

Before leaving he turned around, shook my hand, looked me straight in the eyes, and proclaimed with that dazzling smile: "I'm dying of cancer, but when I crawl out of bed in the morning, I make the most of each living moment. It's like squeezing the juice out of an orange until there's not any left. That's what I'm doing with life right now."

Now O. B. is smiling more broadly than ever as he augments the Heavenly Choir . . . and the Lord helped O. B. to leave a little bit of heaven behind!

Conclusion:
Beating the "Me" Addiction

At one time I was obsessed with being a success. It consumed my thoughts morning, noon, and night. Every day, I had been racing against every moment of every waking hour, struggling to achieve. I couldn't sleep for more than a few hours a night. My mind was preoccupied with planning events and appointments for the following day.

I had only one purpose: making it to the top, even if it killed me. My family and my health were secondary to my being "Number One."

During one of the Midwest's worst droughts, I spent every weekend writing and editing network stories on the unrelenting dry spell. Saturdays and Sundays were packed with interviews, recording sessions, and telephone calls.

At times I would ease up and take one of the boys to a news event. I drove to a nearby lake on July Fourth. Hundreds of vacationers were celebrating Independence Day—fishing, boating, and swimming. There I was with my four-year-old son, Jeffrey. With tape recorder in hand I was interviewing anyone willing to tell me "what the Fourth of July means to me." As I wrapped up the final interview, Jeffrey began to cry. "Oh, Daddy, please—let's stay!" I shot back, "No, Jeff, we don't have time. I've got to send this back right away."

Jeffrey knew, in no uncertain terms, that we were leaving and heading back home. I would spend the rest of the afternoon locked away in my office typing, recording, and relaying the material to the network. My free-lance work had taken priority over my wife and sons. I was a self-induced victim of the "me-myself-and-I" generation.

My painstaking struggles weren't paying off like I wanted. Sure, the family had nice clothes, a new car, and enough money to buy most of what we wanted . . . but there was always an emptiness inside. My patience was wearing thin, and so was my interest in life. I wanted everything "right now," but there never seemed to be enough. After weeks of walking around with all this "stuff" in my head, I was losing touch with my family. The projects I had accepted had become my enemies. They were dominating me. Drowning in the "me" addiction, I was ignoring and hurting those closest to me. I was eaten alive by the "workaholic" syndrome—a quality I thought was essential to a productive, happy existence. But being a workaholic and a me addict make a deadly combination.

When I was engrossed at my desk, I was always too tied up to talk with anyone. "But, Daddy," my sons would protest, "you're always too busy to play with us!"

"You don't understand," I repeatedly reminded them, "I have important things to do. I have to finish them!" I was competing against myself, and there wasn't any part of me left to share with anyone.

Almost none of the books and magazines I was reading emphasized love, compassion, charity, or forgiveness. Being "at the top" was the theme of many best-sellers. "If you spend time thinking about 'making a difference,' " a journalist friend remarked, "quit the news business and become a social worker." I didn't follow his suggestion. Instead, I was eventually able to incorporate the qualities of hundreds of wonderful human beings I had interviewed for radio programs over a period of more than a decade. While I was accumulating their stories, these dynamic people affected my career and my role as a husband and father.

Unfortunately, the "me" generation has professed that "more is better, and better is not enough." A *USA Weekend* review of the movie *Wall Street,* considered a hot picture in 1988, confirmed what I had already been drawn into. The movie's theme was greed and success. One of the actors didn't mince words in the movie: "Greed, for lack of a better word, is good. Greed . . . cuts through to the very essence of what we're doing." In the review, Dr. Robert Reich, a Harvard professor of political economy, was quoted as saying, "For many in this era, riches have supplanted all other goals. In the '60's it was, 'Do your own thing.' In the '70's, it was: 'Looking out for number one.' Now it's 'Money, money, money.' "

George Kettle had it all. In 1981, the rich Northern Virginian controlled a real-estate empire. But, as he later confessed, "I was living a life of desperation." He wanted out!

As he was driving through Pennsylvania, he pulled off the highway. George experienced what he describes as a religious conversion, vowing to pledge 10 percent of his income to do "God's work."

Four years later, he watched a "60 Minutes" feature about a millionaire's promise to send a sixth-grade class to college (of course, years later when they were ready). Kettle, a college drop-out, made a deal with sixty seventh-grade kids in one of Washington, D.C.'s toughest neighborhoods. "Get your high school diploma, and college is on me," the fifty-nine-year old promised them. So far, over one hundred sponsors, including Kettle, have joined the "I Have a Dream" program.

George Kettle has so much in common with the "I Love Life" guests in this book. They have discovered the "other side of life" that isn't popularized by "Wall Street." They have turned thumbs down on the me-myself-and-I syndrome, a life-style that produces heart failure, divorce, depression, and addictions of all sorts.

"You're into One Project—You!"

One evening I arrived home in a grizzly mood, only to have a rude awakening. I had a habit of eating supper and immediately going to my room to type and edit network stories for late-night feeds to the NBC New York Bureau. Without returning downstairs to say "goodnight," I'd turn off the bedroom light when the work was done and attempt to sleep (most of the times, I'd wake up more worn out than when I had retired at night).

Insensitive as I was, I didn't suspect anything was wrong with my family. After all, I was doing what I thought was expected by my wife Linda—provide the necessities and a few luxuries that mány Americans take for granted. *After all,* I convinced myself, *the family will reap the benefits of all my effort.* But, as I soon found out, that didn't concern them.

Without flinching, Linda spelled it out: "Jerry, something's not right. You don't talk to us anymore. You ignore the boys and me. You're into one project: *you!*"

That chilled me to the core! What had I done wrong? After all, wasn't I trying to achieve so they could enjoy more things in life? And now I felt as if my hide were being flayed off.

"You aren't happy, Jerry," Linda went on. "You say you love life, but you don't feel it. You can't sleep at night because you're worried about what you have to do the next day. Unlike the people you interview, you complain about everything that's not part of your plan. Just who are you trying to fool? It's not me or the boys. We just can't go on like this anymore!"

After her verbal avalanche, I figured, *Something has to give, either the relationship or me.* Still, I did not appreciate Linda's lecture. I slinked off to my room. I was furious that my own wife had told me off. *Here am I, trying to make it, and this is all the thanks I get.*

I jerkily grabbed one of the books in my room and began thumbing through it. It wasn't about get-rich schemes or being "number one." This book, *Living, Loving, and Learning* by Leo Buscaglia, was of a different stripe. The chapter I randomly select-ed to read was, for me, more than a coincidence. Buscaglia asked a question that hit me awfully hard: "If I had only five days to live, how would I spend them and with whom?"

That question opened up a new line of thought to me. *Would I be just as messed up then as I am now, consumed by work and goals, or would I have some time to spend laughing and having fun with my wife and boys?—especially if I knew my life would end in a week or even in twenty-four hours?* I put the book down and began thinking and rethinking the question. When I finally dozed off, I actually slept.

As soon as I awoke, my first thought was that question. I made a personal commitment about my family and my life. I marched downstairs and confessed to Linda I was on her side. "I know what you're saying," I admitted. "So, what can I do to show the boys and you?"

After several minutes, she came back with, "The sun's shining, and the wind's blowing. Why not take the boys outside and fly a kite? You've never done it before. Don't expect to get any awards from it or a check from the network. Just relax and have fun with our boys."

That Saturday I dropped my frantic writing and network feeds and gave *myself* to Jeremy and Jeffrey. I gathered in return the love and laughter of my own flesh and blood. It wasn't easy, but their daddy was beating the "me" addiction.

Until that breezy March day, I had been a me person 100 percent. I had taken my family for granted and had become immune to the joys of being a parent and a husband. I had judged all of life by my career. Before this turnaround I was no different from the wealthy multimillionaire caught up in his empire. I had subscribed to the "me" philosophy of life, but it hadn't given me the satisfaction and success I had previously thought it would.

A television newscaster I had known for years had it made, so most of his colleagues thought. Frank (not his actual name) had widespread recognition, a six-figure salary, and career offers from the networks. Everyone at the TV station envied his success. After months of negotiating with a major East Coast television station, Frank signed a contract worth hundreds of thousands of dollars.

Once in the "Top Ten" Eastern market, Frank hit rock bottom as his love affair with alcohol cost him his position. Frank's contract was soon declared null and void. Within months he flew back home and tried to obtain work. By then, the booze was in the driver's seat. Frank put a gun to his head and pulled the trigger— dead at age forty-three. "Success" wasn't enough for Frank.

We tap into the success syndrome and expect happiness right

along with it. But who says there's a guarantee that the two concepts accompany each other? Some of the unhappiest, most depressed, and most miserable human beings are rich and powerful. Sure, they have material possessions, but their lives have no meaning.

An executive with a Christian recording company told me, "The pendulum swings back and forth between materialism and meaning. We search for meaning, and then we realize somehow, for whatever reason, that it's more fun to be rich. And then there's this great search toward MBA degrees. Kids in high school now want to take business classes more than ever before. And then, once everybody learns how to make money hand over fist, they feel this void in their lives. And they go back and search for meaning.

"Just look in the media," he continued, There's a great hunger in America for meaning. We figured out how to make money again. The yuppies have come. They've got their MBA degrees, and now they're searching for meaning."

An article in the January 1988 *Better Homes and Gardens* revealed the results of a questionnaire about spirituality and religion. Of eighty-thousand respondents, 50 percent thought that spirituality was gaining influence on family life in America. Many of them noted that through their religious and spiritual pursuits, "they have gained the strength and grace to withstand tragedy and adversity."

Why "I Love Life"!

I've been blessed this past decade. The "I Love Life" guests have given me the incentive and opportunity to write and broadcast their stories. They have provided my listeners and me a unique perspective of real achievement and success. Instead of sitting at home with the shades drawn and wallowing in misery with a "poor-me" facial expression, each of them has ridden the waves of adversity and challenge and, in their own ways, have triumphed.

I have benefited from them. When I had an opportunity to leave my hometown in the Midwest and relocate in Nashville, I kept thinking, *What if I fail, and it doesn't work out? What if it's not what I really want?* On the outside, I portrayed a successful, award-winning reporter cited in the Congressional Record as an "outstanding" newsman and a respected member of the community. But within me, I was running scared. I was fearful of change. Instead of admitting to anyone at first, I kept it to myself. That was a mistake. I was a victim of "security."

I easily identified with an article, "Searching for Security," written by Aris Whitman. What I was experiencing was not uncommon. Whitman summed it up:

> We feel much safer when everything is familiar—the house we've lived in for years, the job we know so much about, the people whose reactions we can count on, the rituals we've repeated year after year and the ideas we've long believed in. If we resist change, we're like the rigidly built structures that are the first to come down in an earthquake.

I was scared of change, and I would not dare admit my fears to anyone anywhere. To do so would have been a sign of weakness —at least I presumed it was. Yet, I wanted badly to take a leap of faith and accept another position elsewhere. But the "what if's?" stopped me cold. *What if I can't make it in another market? What if I hate the next town and can't handle the job? What if . . .? After all, the older you are in this business, the tougher it is to find work.*

My fear of failure prevented me from leaving the so-called "secure" career I had built for myself. But, as Whitman pointed out, one's false sense of security can easily be destroyed. I understood what she meant, but reading books and magazines was much easier than the stark reality of telling myself, "Yes, I will accept the position." That meant risk, and my mind was reasoning, *You may hate where you are, but at least you're playing it safe.*

In this respect I was like many of my friends in the broadcasting business. They dodged opportunities offered them. Instead of going for it, they were kept back by the what if's? They decided to remain where they were—unhappy and disenchanted with their careers and life. One of them believed, "If you're past thirty, forget it. Stay where you are." That advice was very disheartening since I had already passed the "big three-oh."

Instead of driving myself into a panic, I called one of the "I Love Life" guests, who was also a friend. I wanted to confide in her about my fears. Perhaps I even wanted her to tell me, "Stay here. Why rock the boat and take the risk of losing everything?" Rae Unzicker, who had overcome unbearable obstacles of her own as a former mental patient, invited me to her home. "Let's talk before you go crazy," she suggested.

As we sat together in her office, Rae was aware of my frustrations. "You need to move," she strongly advised me. "You'll grow and mature and even know yourself better. Make it an adventure like a ship heading into unknown waters. It should be exciting. Change always is."

"But, Rae," I questioned. "I've lived here for a long time. Why take a chance and go somewhere else to start all over again? Linda and I have a great doctor, a lawyer we trust, a wonderful church." On and on I listed my reasons for staying put.

"Jerry," she reacted, "don't be afraid of change. Each of our lives can end so quickly. If you have an opportunity, don't say no just because you're accustomed to the place where you live. You need to launch out. Trust me. You'll survive."

When I reached home I prayed again and again for support and guidance. "Please, Lord," I inquired, "What should I do with my life? I'm so afraid of moving and then failing. What should I do?"

Linda and I spent many hours together discussing the move. "If you don't succeed," Linda confidently told me, "I'll work, and you can take care of the kids."

If you have read this far—or even skipped around in this book —you know the story. We made the move. After several years in Nashville, we have rediscovered each other. As I was finishing this book, our third son, Aaron, was born. Away from our families in the Midwest, Linda and I have been drawn closer together than ever before. We are not only husband and wife but friends who freely talk with each other. Stepping out together on faith, Linda and I have learned, can make a marriage and family stronger—and both partners more confident of their abilities.

Thanks to Rae, I have grown, and so has "I Love Life." The move to Nashville has meant more than a new position. For the first time in years we found hope for our son Jeremy (through his treatments at Vanderbilt University Medical Center). I have gathered a harvest of inspiration from inimitable people I never would have known if we had not dared to move here. People like George Allen, Nancy McDaniel, the Strobel brothers, Nadine Zemba, and the other "I Love Life" guests are not merely interview subjects. They are friends who have accepted me into their lives—and have enriched and ennobled my life, along with the lives of thousands of others.

It is an honor to share their stories with you. I can only hope they have touched you, as they have me, and that, in spite of your ups and downs, highs and lows, you will be able to exclaim . . . .

"I LOVE LIFE!"

CHRISTIAN HERALD
People Making a Difference

Christian Herald is a family of dedicated, Christ-centered ministries that reaches out to deprived children in need, and to homeless men who are lost in alcoholism and drug addiction. Christian Herald also offers the finest in family and evangelical literature through its book club and publishes a popular, dynamic magazine for today's Christians.

Our Ministries

Christian Herald Children. The door of God's grace opens wide to give impoverished youngsters a breath of fresh air, away from the evils of the streets. Every summer, hundreds of youngsters are welcomed at the Christian Herald Mont Lawn Camp located in the Poconos at Bushkill, Pennsylvania. Year-round assistance is also provided, including teen programs, tutoring in reading and writing, family counseling, career guidance and college scholarship programs.

The Bowery Mission. Located in New York City, the Bowery Mission offers hope and Gospel strength to the downtrodden and homeless. Here, the men of Skid Row are fed, clothed, ministered to. Many voluntarily enter a 6-month discipleship program of spiritual guidance, nutrition therapy and Bible study.

Our Father's House. Our Father's House is a discipleship program located in a rural setting in Lancaster County, Pennsylvania, which enables addicts to take the last steps on the road to a useful Christian life.

Paradise Lake Retreat Center. During the spring, fall and winter months, our children's camp at Bushkill, Pennsylvania, becomes a lovely retreat for religious gatherings of up to 200. Excellent accommodations include an on-site chapel, heated cabins, large meeting areas, recreational facilities, and delicious country-style meals. Write to: Paradise Lake Retreat Center, Box 252, Bushkill, PA 18234, or call: (717) 588-6067.

Christian Herald Magazine is contemporary—a dynamic publication that addresses the vital concerns of today's Christian. Each issue contains a sharing of true personal stories written by people who have found in Christ the strength to make a difference in the world around them.

Family Bookshelf provides a wide selection of wholesome, inspirational reading and Christian literature written by best-selling authors. All books are recommended by an Advisory Board of distinguished writers and editors.

* * *

Christian Herald ministries, founded in 1878, are supported by the voluntary contributions of individuals and by legacies and bequests. Contributions are tax deductible. Checks should be made out to: Christian Herald Children, Bowery Mission, or Christian Herald Association.

Fully-accredited Member
of the Evangelical Council
for Financial Accountability

Administrative Office:
40 Overlook Drive
Chappaqua, New York 10514
Telephone: (914) 769-9000